ISO27001 in a Windows® Environment

The best practice handbook for a Microsoft® Windows® environment

Third edition

ISO27001 in a Windows® Environment

The best practice handbook for a Microsoft® Windows® environment

Third edition

BRIAN HONAN

IT Governance Publishing

IT Governance Publishing
IT Governance Limited
Unit 3, Clive Court
Bartholomew's Walk
Cambridgeshire Business Park
Ely, Cambridgeshire
CB7 4EA
United Kingdom
www.itgovernance.co.uk

First published in the United Kingdom in 2009
by IT Governance Publishing.

ISBN 978-1-905356-78-2

Second edition published in 2010.
ISBN 978-1-84928-049-5

Third edition published in 2014.
ISBN 978-1-84928-603-9

FOREWORD

The standard for Information Security Management Systems (ISMS), ISO/IEC 27001, provides a significant implementation challenge for all organisations. ISO27001 is a management standard: it sets out a specification for how management should identify, from a business risk perspective, the controls and safeguards that should be applied to information assets in order to assure their confidentiality, integrity and confidentiality. Management – and also the ISMS implementation project manager – will usually have a general or quality management background.

A significant number of the controls to be applied will, of necessity, be technical and will relate to how IT hardware and software are set up and configured. The technical knowledge to carry out this configuration is usually within the IT or corporate information security team and, because information security is a business responsibility, this team should never have overall accountability for determining the actual controls required by the ISMS.

As a result, there is often a gulf in understanding as to what is required between the ISO27001 ISMS project manager and those responsible for implementing the technical controls. This book does an outstanding job of helping parties on both sides to bridge the gulf. It identifies the recommended technical controls of ISO27001's Annex A and, for a Microsoft environment, provides guidance on how (if, on the basis of a risk assessment, they are considered necessary) to implement them.

This book fills a major hole in the guidance literature for ISO27001 and will make a significant contribution to helping both project managers and IT and security staff get to grips with what controls are appropriate to mitigate identified risks.

While this book covers implementations in a wide range of Windows® environments, this third edition is completely up to date for Windows® 8 and Server® 2012. This book is so useful that it should be a core part of every information security professional's library.

Alan Calder

June 2014

PREFACE

This book is the culmination of my work with various clients in implementing their ISO27001 information security management systems. Having watched clients struggle to understand and grasp the concepts of ISO27001 and then having to further translate those concepts so that their technical IT personnel could appreciate what was required, I decided to write this book to make that task easier for them.

I also decided that since the Microsoft® Windows® platform and various other Microsoft products are so commonly used in many organisations, I would base the technical details on those Microsoft technologies.

So began a long and interesting journey as I delved further into the workings of Microsoft® Windows® 7, Microsoft® Windows Server® 2008 and various other products. (And, since then, I have updated this book to account for newer products including, crucially, Microsoft® Windows® 8 and Microsoft® Windows Server® 2012.) My goal was to identify how an IT Manager could leverage the Microsoft technology already available to them to support their implementation of the ISO27001 information security management standard.

That journey brought me into contact for the first time with the numerous tools, utilities and products that Microsoft provides, which can be readily applied to most environments and to which I will introduce you in this book.

Preface

This book is designed as a step-by-step guide through the journey of implementing ISO27001 in a Microsoft® Windows® environment. You can choose to read the book in a linear fashion from the first to the last page as a companion for your ISO27001 journey, or it can be used as a reference guide to which you can refer when you need to verify a control or associated technical setting.

Approached in the right way, the journey to achieving certification to the ISO27001 information security management standard can be smooth, without too many bumps, twists or turns. Using this book will assist you on that journey, providing you with a roadmap and signposts along the way to get to your destination.

ABOUT THE AUTHOR

Brian Honan is recognised as an industry expert on information security, in particular the ISO27001 information security standard, and has addressed a number of major conferences relating to the management and securing of information technology.

An independent consultant based in Dublin, Ireland, Brian provides consulting services to clients in various industry segments and his work also includes advising various Government security agencies and the European Commission. Brian also established Ireland's first ever Computer Security Incident Response Team.

Brian is also an Adjunct lecturer at University College Dublin lecturing on Information Security Management.

In 2013, Brian was appointed as a special advisor on Internet Security to Europol's Cybercrime Centre

He has also had a number of technical papers published and has been technical editor and reviewer of a number of industry-recognised publications. Brian is also the European editor for the SANS Institute's weekly SANS NewsBites, a semi-weekly electronic newsletter.

He is a member of the Irish Information Security Forum, Information Systems Audit and Control Association, and a member of the Irish Computer Society, and is president of the Irish Chapter of the Cloud Security Alliance.

x

ACKNOWLEDGEMENTS

This book would not have been possible without the support of many people. They provided encouragement and guidance from the concept of this book to its final publication. For fear of forgetting to mention anyone I shall not list them here.

There is one person, though, without whose help and support I would not have been able to complete this book, my wife, Veronica. She provided me with encouragement when I needed it, scolding when I deserved it and time and space when required. For all that, and much more, she will always have my undying love and appreciation.

CONTENTS

Contents

Contents

INTRODUCTION

Information security, once viewed as being solely within the domain of the IT department, is now a key issue for many businesses and organisations. Industry regulations, legal requirements, media coverage of information security incidents and a growing demand from clients that companies better manage and secure the information within their care have forced information security out of the IT department and into the boardroom.

Companies are now faced with the dilemma of ensuring their information is secure enough to satisfy their business needs and is also compliant with various legal and regulatory requirements, such as the Data Protection Act, Basel II and III, or the US Sarbanes-Oxley Act.

Information security is not solely about compliance, demonstrating best practices or implementing the latest technical solutions. It is about managing the risks posed to the business by the accidental or deliberate misuse of confidential information. It is important to note that no matter what the industry, whether in the private or public sector, every organisation has confidential information it needs to protect. This information could be customer details, payroll information, credit-card numbers, business plans, financial information or intellectual property, to name but a few examples.

The problem many companies face is that there are no recommended benchmarks or minimum grades clearly stated in most of the compliance regulations they need to meet and the business is often not clear about what it requires. Those faced with the responsibility of securing a company's information are confronted with the onerous task of trying to determine how best to implement effective security controls for their systems and information, without any clear guidance on what constitutes legal compliance.[1]

The ISO27001 information security standard offers companies a way to address this problem. Originally known as BS7799 part 2, ISO27001 is a vendor and technology-neutral internationally recognised standard that provides companies with a risk-based approach to securing their information assets.

ISO27001 certification provides organisations with independent third-party verification that their information security management system (ISMS) meets an internationally recognised standard. This provides a company, and its employees, customers and partners, with the confidence that it is managing its security in accordance with recognised and audited best practices.

By adopting the risk- and standards-based approach to implementing an ISMS in accordance with ISO27001, you can reap many advantages, not least of being better able to demonstrate compliance with legal and industry regulatory requirements.

It is important to note that the ISO27001 information security standard can simply be used as a framework against which a company can implement and measure its ISMS, without necessarily having to be accredited. This is particularly useful for companies wishing to ensure they are

---

[1] Read *Information Security Law: The Emerging Standard for Corporate Compliance,* Smedinghoff T, ITGP (2008) for guidance on this issue.

implementing an effective ISMS but without necessarily wanting full certification to the standard.

However, implementing ISO27001 can be a challenge for many organisations. While the standard is prescriptive in terms of the management system, it is not prescriptive about the controls that must be implemented; nor does it provide a checklist of items that an organisation can tick off to be secure against all relevant risks.

So, after the business has decided that the ISO27001 information security standard will enable it to meet its information security requirements, very often the task of implementing the standard falls to the IT Manager. This can be a major challenge for them as they must first become familiar with ISO27001 and interpret it in accordance with their organisation's unique business requirements and risk profile, while ensuring that any controls that are identified are properly implemented.

This book is designed to assist the IT Manager along the road to successfully implementing the ISO27001 information security standard by introducing them to the concept of what an ISMS is and how to use ISO27001 to ensure its quality.

Once the IT Manager understands the requirements of an ISMS, the book will then describe the various inbuilt features within Microsoft's current family of server and desktop operating systems and some additional products, which can be employed to support the ISMS. This book focuses primarily on Microsoft technologies as they are so predominant in many business environments. By employing the native features of the Windows® operating systems, and some additional complementary Microsoft products, this book will demonstrate how certification against ISO27001 can be achieved. As most of the technologies are already built into the Microsoft platform, it should be possible for an organisation to achieve certification without having to purchase additional third-party software products.

Finally, this book will also provide technical details on what IT technicians should be considering to ensure that the controls identified as necessary are in place and are effective.

CHAPTER 1: INFORMATION AND INFORMATION SECURITY

Before we begin our ISO27001 journey, it is important that we understand what it is that we are trying to achieve. When most people hear the phrase information security, they automatically think that it is applicable only to IT and the securing of computers and networks.

But information can take many forms and is not only bits and bytes on computers or networks. Information can be printed or written on to paper; it can be verbal, whether spoken face to face, in a crowded room or over a telephone; or it can indeed be stored or transmitted electronically by computers, networks or fax machines.

Information is considered to be one of the most valuable assets a company can have. Customer databases, business plans and intellectual property are just some examples of how information becomes the lifeblood of many organisations. Without the correct information, senior management may make the wrong strategic decisions; information in the hands of a competitor could undermine a company's competitiveness; or information lost from a laptop or a briefcase, or accessed by unauthorised people, could expose sensitive customer data, leaving the organisation facing negative publicity and, in some cases, serious fines.

Therefore it is important that we take steps to protect information when it is being transmitted, exchanged or stored, whatever format it is in.

This is where information security comes into play. When we speak about information security, what we are actually talking about is how we prevent security incidents and minimise their impact on the business. To do this we need to understand the various information security concepts.

Information security concepts

To better understand information security, there are a number of concepts that you should keep in mind when considering what controls to put in place to secure information. In the context of the ISO27001 information security standard, there are three core concepts that we need to consider when designing our controls or measures to protect our information. Widely referred to as the CIA of information security, these are specifically:

- Confidentiality
- Integrity
- Availability.

Confidentiality is where we ensure that information is only available to the appropriate individuals.

Integrity is ensuring that the information has not been altered in any way, either deliberately or accidentally.

Availability is how we ensure that the information can be accessed by those (and only by those) with the appropriate permissions.

Other information security concepts

While the CIA concepts are widely viewed as the three pillars upon which to build your information security, there are a number of other concepts that we should also keep in mind:

- **Identification:** This involves the mechanisms we would put in place to identify a user to a system; for example, their photo on an ID card or their unique user ID to log on to a network.
- **Authentication:** This is the means of proving that an individual is who they claim to be. This could be a security guard checking the picture on an ID card is that of the person holding the card, or a secret password to match the person's unique user ID.
- **Authorisation:** Once a person has been identified and authenticated, we then need to ensure they have the appropriate authorisation to do what they need to do. We could restrict an individual to access only certain folders on the network by using network permissions on the files, or restrict physical access by only allowing their swipe card to open certain doors in the building.
- **Accountability:** It is important that we can identify what an individual has done once they have access to a system or an environment. Computer security logs and audit trails can record what a person does when authenticated to a system or a closed-circuit TV system could be used to record who accesses certain parts of the premises.
- **Privacy:** This concept relates both to the fundamentals of the confidentiality of the company's data and to the protection of the privacy of those who use the systems.
- **Non-repudiation:** Non-repudiation is where we can prove that a particular action or transaction was completed by a specific individual; for example, a signature on a cheque or someone signing a contract, making it impossible to repudiate that contract.

- **Reliability:** Any action or behaviour should be consistent, so a consistent action should produce consistent results. For instance, the processes involved in providing authorisation should always give the same user the same authority.

The importance of information security

As stated earlier, information is probably one of the most valuable assets a company can hold; however, as information is intangible, the value of it can often be overlooked. Unlike stock, factory machinery or company premises, information is not very visible to an organisation even though it sits on every desk, in every computer and in every filing cabinet. This can make it difficult for organisations to fully appreciate its value and implement the appropriate protections.

Information security should therefore be driven by the business needs of the organisation as it must at all times take these into account. Rather than being a technical issue, information security is clearly a management and governance issue and one that must be driven by senior management.

As economies become more and more global, companies are relying more and more on information for the success, and indeed the survival, of their business. New business channels are being facilitated by the Internet and related technologies, allowing many businesses to communicate more directly and effectively with customers, staff, partners and suppliers.

Companies can now expand into global markets using online websites, customer service is better facilitated by the use of email and instant messaging, and Voice over IP provides cost-effective voice communications. Cooperation with partners and providers is better facilitated by the same technologies and online banking allows for payments to be sent and received faster and far more efficiently than before.

All of the above technologies provide us with ways and means for transmitting, storing and processing information more efficiently. While all of the above provide many advantages to businesses, they also bring with them a greater dependency on the underlying technologies. Any interruptions, be they accidental or deliberate, can have a major impact on a business. Prolonged outages whereby information is not available or issues that result in the information becoming corrupted can have a significant impact on the bottom line of any business.

In addition to the above, most of the technologies that we use to process our information with third parties, customers or remote staff are based on the Internet. The Internet is a collection of networks that are interconnected and the Internet is not policed nor managed by any one entity. This can lead to variances in the quality and security of service that can be experienced as information travels from one point to another.

Against this backdrop, the IT Manager is also challenged with minimising the amount of system down time while at the same time maintaining the competitive advantage these technologies provide to the business.

All of the information processing facilities, be they technical or human based, need to comply with various regulatory and legal requirements. For some industries, e.g. financial and health care, certain types of information need to be stored and archived in particular formats for predefined periods of time. At all times the legal framework within which an organisation operates has to be complied with, e.g. the EU Data Protection Directive. These issues become more and more of a challenge as an organisation grows its operations globally and operates or deals with customers in different countries, resulting in having to comply with various local laws and regulations.

The IT Manager is often tasked with ensuring the above business security requirements are met while at the same time having to manage everything within an ever-dwindling IT budget.

CHAPTER 2: USING AN ISMS TO COUNTER THE THREATS

According to the International Organization for Standardization (ISO), the developers of ISO27001, an information security management system 'is a systematic approach to managing sensitive company information so that it remains secure. It includes people, processes and IT systems by applying a risk management process'. Simply put, an ISMS is a framework which management employs to ensure a structured approach is taken to identify the business risks posed against key information assets and how best to manage, eliminate or mitigate those risks.

An effective ISMS will be an integrated part of the overall management system within a company. This is to ensure that senior management is involved and is committed to the ISMS. As with all major initiatives, senior management commitment is critical to ensuring the success of your ISMS. Without such commitment, you will be left fighting to justify the controls you wish to implement; having senior management commitment makes this task a lot easier.

An effective ISMS is based on taking a business-risk approach to establishing, implementing, operating and monitoring the ISMS. It is important to maintain focus on the business requirements at all times. A successful ISMS should not be seen as a barrier to conducting business but rather as a tool to enable the business to meet its goals in a secure manner.

Information security management systems are often likened to the brakes on a car. While brakes are often viewed as a means to stop a car, they are in effect key safety features on the car that allow the driver to get to their destination safely. Without brakes on a car, the car would crash or the journey would take much longer as the driver would have to drive very slowly to ensure they encountered no accidents. Whereas with brakes on the car, the driver can negotiate twists and turns in the road much more effectively and get to their destination much more quickly and safely. Similarly, an effective ISMS should not prevent a business achieving certain goals but ensure the business can achieve those goals in as safe and secure manner as possible, without any misfortunes happening along that journey.

System security versus information security

It is important that we remind ourselves at all times what the difference between information security and system security is.

System, or IT, security focuses primarily on the technologies, such as networks, computers and applications that are used to create, modify or transfer our information assets. Therefore the focus of system security is very much at the technical end of the spectrum and includes solutions, such as intrusion detection systems, anti-virus software, cryptography and firewalls amongst others.

Information security, on the other hand, focuses on how information is protected and concentrates mainly on managerial and business solutions. System security has a place in information security but is simply another part of the information security management solution together with items, such as policies, procedures, people, legal issues, and the security culture of the organisation, the policies and the organisation's approach to risk.

Information security is therefore a much more holistic approach than system security in protecting the information assets of an organisation and ensures that risks to the organisation's information assets are identified, quantified and managed.

The structure of an ISMS

An ISMS is a management system that is put in place to ensure that all safeguards implemented to protect an organisation's information assets are appropriate, operating as expected and providing feedback on ways to continuously improve the ISMS.

A successful ISMS will provide a risk-based framework that contains a number of core elements which will ensure a systematic approach to managing an organisation's sensitive information so that it remains secure. The ISMS is dependent on people understanding their roles within the system and being aware of their responsibilities. It cannot be stressed strongly enough that the ISMS will only succeed if it has the commitment of senior management within the organisation. Without this commitment, the training and awareness required to be given to staff may not be forthcoming, resulting in an ineffective ISMS.

Information security policy

The cornerstone to any successful ISMS is the information security policy. This document drives the whole system and sets the framework for decisions on what controls, be they human, technical or procedural, need to be put in place.

An effective information security policy will align itself with the business needs of the organisation, but at the same time it must take into account the culture and security needs of the organisation in question. An information security policy for a branch of the security services may be much more security focused than, say, a policy for a small business.

It is important that the information security policy balances the levels of security controls with levels of productivity. If the security controls become too intrusive into how people do their jobs, they will invariably ignore or bypass the controls, making the policy ineffective.

To ensure buy-in to the information security policy, a number of people should be consulted regarding its structure and content. Senior management should give their input to the policy and ensure that it is aligned with the requirements of the business. Representatives of the end-users should also be consulted to ensure that the policy will be accepted by staff. Company lawyers and auditors should also be involved with the design of the policy to ensure that it complies with any legal, regulatory or contractual requirements, and that the auditors are familiar with the policy in order to facilitate future audits.

It is also prudent to involve representatives from IT in the policy design process. While the policy should not be a technically focused document, it is important that IT are aware of the implications of what is being proposed by the policy so as to ensure that technical controls can be implemented where required and monitoring solutions implemented to assist in the management and enforcement of the policy.

When developing the information security policy, you should ensure it remains concise and easy to understand. The most successful policies are those that are written in plain language, avoiding legal jargon. It is also important that you include within the information security policy the reasons why it is needed and what exactly is covered by the policy, explain how violations will be dealt with and detail the main roles and responsibilities for information security.

The information security policy should be designed with the size of the organisation in mind. Some organisations may have one policy to cover all information security issues whereas other organisations may have multiple policies to cover specific areas of information security.

The decision to have either a single comprehensive information security policy or a number of smaller policies can be influenced by issues, such as the number of sites within your organisation, the types of business units, the different types of workforce that you may have or indeed the structure of your organisation.

Whether you decide to use one single policy or multiple policies, it is important that they meet the requirements of ISO27001. They should also refer to the following, secondary policies.

Acceptable usage policy

This policy discusses the appropriate usage of the organisation's computing resources. It is essential that all users read and accept this policy before they are allowed to access any of the organisation's computer systems. Ideally this policy should not be technology specific; otherwise you may end up constantly having to update the policy or it will be superseded by newer technologies.

Remote access policy

In order to ensure that all connections to your internal network are managed in the most appropriate manner, a remote access policy should outline and define the acceptable methods for remote users, such as road warriors, homeworkers and third parties, to connect to the network. Again the policy should be technology neutral and highlight who has the authority, and under what conditions, to grant remote access to people or other organisations.

Information management policy

Your information management policy should provide guidance to users on how they should handle and manage information with regards to its classification. For example, information that is sensitive should be dealt with differently to information that would be available to the public. The main goal of the information management policy should be to ensure that information is appropriately protected from modification and/or disclosure.

Computer malware prevention and protection policy

This policy should detail what the requirements are for protecting your systems from infection from computer malware, such as computer viruses, Trojans, spyware and keyloggers. While most of the controls in place will be technical, it is important that you keep this policy technology and/or product neutral so that the goals of the policy can adapt to new threats as they arise. The policy should detail what protections need to be installed on the end-user workstations, servers, the network and your network ingress and egress points. Other mechanisms that can be used to transport malicious software into your organisation should also be included, such as Internet downloads, USB keys, CDs, DVDs and floppy disks. The policy should detail how often the software should be deployed, maintained and updated. Guidelines on how to report and contain suspected virus outbreaks should also be included. Ideally you should also integrate this policy with your incident response and business continuity policies.

Password policy

Your password policy should detail the minimum requirements your organisation requires for all passwords, be they user, system or vendor passwords. It should include the rules relating to creating passwords, such as their length, how often they expire, whether the passwords are complex and their uniqueness. The password policy should clearly state how individuals should protect their passwords from disclosure and what to do in the event that this should happen.

Your policies will form the cornerstone of the rest of your ISMS. The key to successful policies is keeping them simple and easily understood. The best policies tend to be short, to the point, relevant and easy to read. Remember that your policies are the main drivers for identifying what processes, procedures, and personal and technical controls you may need to implement to support the policy.

Therefore it is important to remember that policies should very rarely change and should be written in a language that is technology agnostic and should refer to titles and roles rather than individuals.

Your processes and procedures can be more detailed and technically specific as these can be changed as required.

It may help to think of your policies as being the equivalent of a country's constitution while the processes and procedures are the laws to support the constitution. Constitutions rarely get changed as they define the goals while laws are implemented and amended as required.

Managing exceptions to the policy

You should also remember that with all your policies there will no doubt be some exceptions. There will be new technologies or new business requirements that may not comply with the policy. You and your senior management will need to be able to manage such exceptions by conducting a risk assessment to see whether the exception requires the policy to be amended to accommodate it or whether to accept and manage the risk posed by the exception to the policy. For example, the business may require a new application to be installed on the network to enable it to branch into a new market. However, that application's inbuilt password management system may not comply with your own password policy. You may recall from earlier in this chapter that information security should facilitate business and not be seen as a barrier to it. As a result, you should approach senior management and highlight the risks posed by this new application being introduced into the organisation and the controls you propose to manage the risk. Senior management can then make a business decision based on the risk assessment provided, and either authorise the exception, require that policies are amended to support it, or reject the application as it may pose too great a risk to the organisation.

CHAPTER 3: AN INTRODUCTION TO ISO27001

The ISO27000 family of standards, similar to the ISO9000 family of quality standards, provides a series of information security standards of which the ISO27001 information security standard is just one.

The ISO27001 information security standard is a management system specification that provides organisations with an internationally recognised best-practice standard against which independent third-party verification of conformance can be provided. This provides an organisation, and its customers and partners, with the confidence that it is managing its security in accordance with recognised and audited best practices.

The ISO27001 information security standard is a standard against which an organisation can certify its ISMS. Note that certification is optional as organisations can simply decide to use the standard as a framework against which they can build their ISMS. Certification does have the advantage of providing an organisation with independent third-party verification that their ISMS is effective and operating to a documented standard.

The ISO27001 information security standard has been developed to meet the information security needs of organisations of all types and sizes. It is ideal for any organisation that wants to demonstrate that it manages its information security to an internationally recognised set of standards.

It is important to remember that ISO27001 covers all types of information and is therefore not limited to technology.

The standard does not provide you with a checklist of items that you can implement to make your information systems secure. Instead, the controls you select are dependent on your own risk assessment, which in turn is dependent on your organisation.

By adopting a risk- and standards-based approach to implementing an ISMS in accordance with ISO27001, organisations can reap many advantages, not least being better able to demonstrate compliance with legal and industry regulatory requirements.

The ISO27000 standards family

The ISO27000 family of information security standards includes a number of standards that are already publicised or are currently in development.

Table 1 lists the main standards that are members of the ISO27000 standards family. Note that, at the time of writing, not all of these standards have been published.

Table 1: ISO27000 standards

Standard	Description	Published
ISO27000	Will provide an overview of the ISO27000 standards and also provide a definition of terms and vocabulary used within the standards.	2012
ISO27001	This standard is the ISMS requirements standard against which organisations are certified.	2013

ISO27002	Provides the code of practice for information security management. This standard describes the objectives of the information security controls using generally accepted best-practice guidelines for information security.	2013
ISO27003	This standard provides a set of guidelines for those wishing to implement the ISO27000 family of standards.	2010
ISO27004	Provides a set of metrics or measurements to measure the efficiency or otherwise of the ISMS.	2009
ISO27005	This standard provides guidance on conducting information security risk management. Note that this standard does not specify any particular methodology as a preferred solution.	2011
ISO27006	Provides guidelines to the various certification bodies on the process for certifying other organisations' ISMSs.	2011
ISO27007	Provides those who audit ISMSs against the ISO27001 information security standard with guidelines on how best to do so.	2011

History of ISO27001

The ISO27001 standard has a long history and has taken a number of forms during its development.

It originally appeared as the 'Users' Code of Practice' published by the United Kingdom's Department of Trade and Industry's Commercial Computer Security Centre (CCSC) in 1989. A number of representatives from British industry and the United Kingdom's National Computer Centre developed the 'Users' Code of Practice' further and published the British Standard's guidance document 'PD0003 – A Code of Practice for Information Security Management', which was released in 1993.

After a period of additional consultation, the British Standards Institute then revised 'A Code of Practice for Information Security Management' and released it as BS7799-1:1995.

In 1998, the British Standards Institute added a second part to the standard; this was known as BS7799-2:1998.

The British Standards Institute had begun another review and public consultation process in 1997 and as a result updated and published BS7799 Part 1 in 1999 (BS7799-1:1999). BS7799-1:1999 was fast-tracked as an ISO/IEC standard and was published in 2000 as ISO/IEC 17799:2000, which in turn has now become ISO/IEC 27002:2005. This was originally released as ISO/IEC 17799:2005 and reissued under the intended nomenclature of ISO27002:2005 in 2008.

The standard known as BS7799-2:1998 was, after a number of other updates and revisions, released as BS7799-2:2002 in 2002. In 2005, the BS7799-2:2002 information security standard was entered into the ISO/IEC fast-track mechanism and towards the end of that year it was released as ISO/IEC 27001:2005.

In 2013, both ISO/IEC 27001 and ISO/IEC 27002 were revised. This revision took into account new developments in information security and feedback from organisations that had implemented the standards, and amended some requirements to simplify the process of implementing an ISMS.

What is in the ISO27001 standard?

The ISO27001 information security standard is the one standard among the ISO27000 family of standards against which an organisation's ISMS can be audited and certified. The goal of the ISO27001 standard is to 'provide a model for establishing, implementing, operating, monitoring, reviewing, maintaining, and improving an information security management system'.

The ISO27001 information security standard specifies a number of requirements that an organisation's ISMS must meet in order to comply with the standard. The main body of the standard describes the mandatory elements of the ISMS. The requirement for a company to conduct a risk assessment, and base its selection of controls on the outcome of that risk assessment, is an essential and fundamental part of the standard. Appendix A of ISO27001 consists of 14 control sections, 35 control objectives and 114 individual controls. The 14 control sections are broken down as follows:

- **Information security policies:** This section of the standard is to ensure that management provide direction and support for information security in the organisation.

- **Organization of information security:** In order to help you manage information security within the organisation, this section outlines a number of controls that relate to the organisation of information security, including contact with external parties.
- **Human resources security:** As humans are such a large factor in information security, this section contains controls that aim to reduce the risks of human error, theft, fraud or misuse of facilities.
- **Asset management:** Asset management focuses on identifying your information assets and protecting them appropriately.
- **Access control:** As information is the core asset secured by ISO27001, this section contains controls that secure and manage access to information assets.
- **Cryptography:** This section provides controls to manage both the use of cryptography and the management of cryptographic keys.
- **Physical and environmental security:** This section contains controls to prevent unauthorised access, damage and interference to business premises and information assets.
- **Operations security:** This section provides controls to protect day-to-day business operations, such as through the standardisation of overarching processes (change management, for instance), protection from malware, audit logging, software management, and so on.
- **Communications security:** This section contains controls to ensure the correct and secure operation of information processing facilities.
- **System acquisition, development and maintenance:** This section of the ISO27001 information security standard has a number of controls to ensure that security

is built into information systems, whether they are developed in-house or by third parties, or are commercial off-the-shelf software packages.

- **Supplier relationships:** Organisations almost inevitably do business with other organisations, and information security must be preserved throughout this process. This section provides controls to ensure that information security is established throughout the supply chain.
- **Information security incident management:** Invariably there will be breaches of information security controls, and this section of the standard concentrates on how all information security events and weaknesses can be reported and responded to effectively.
- **Information security aspects of business continuity management:** To counteract interruptions to business activities and to protect critical business processes from the effects of major failures or disasters, this section highlights controls to be put in place in respect of the information security aspects of business continuity.
- **Compliance:** This section contains controls designed to help organisations avoid breaches of any criminal or civil law, statutory, regulatory or contractual obligations, and any security requirement.

Continual improvement

In the field of information security, it is important that the controls within your ISMS are constantly updated to cope with new threats posed by changes in business conditions, new technologies or advances in existing technologies. ISO27001 requires you to continually improve the ISMS, and through this process ensure that the controls selected are appropriate, effective and efficient.

In its previous incarnation, ISO27001 required the organisation to ensure that the ISMS was regularly improved using the Plan-Do-Check-Act cycle (PDCA). With the 2013 revision, however, this requirement has been modified such that PDCA is no longer the mandated methodology for continual improvement.

While PDCA is a straightforward and well recognised model for continual improvement, some organisations may have had difficulty in implementing it due to larger scale business decisions, contractual obligations or, in some cases, legislative requirements. For organisations required to use methodologies such as COBIT® or ITIL®, for instance, which include defined models for continual improvement, being required to "plug in" a different methodology was a procedural headache.

Additionally, by relieving the organisation of this requirement, the Standard allows you to use a model best suited to your business needs. Whether this is a proven methodology like the seven-stage continual improvement cycle established in COBIT® or the Continuous Service Improvement (CSI) used in ITIL®, or even a model designed internally to match the organisation's goals, size and complexity, ISO27001 only requires that the organisation "continually improve the suitability, adequacy and effectiveness of the information security management system."[2]

---

[2] ISO/IEC 27001:2013, Clause 10.2.

What are the benefits of ISO27001?

A challenge facing companies that are considering implementing an ISMS is quantifying the benefits that can be derived from it. While tangible results can be demonstrated from investing in new hardware or in staff, it can be quite difficult to demonstrate to senior management the benefits from investing time, resources and money in an ISMS.

However, companies that have implemented an ISO27001-based ISMS can demonstrate many efficiencies and other benefits, such as the following:

- **Increased reliability and security of systems:** Using an independent and international standard-based approach, which ensures that adequate controls, processes and procedures are in place, will ensure the CIA goals of security will be met and also, by default, improve the reliability, availability and stability of systems.
- **Increased profits:** Having stable, secure and reliable systems ensures that interruptions to those systems are minimised, thereby increasing their availability and productivity. In addition to the above, a standards-based approach to information security demonstrates to customers that the company can be trusted with their business. This can increase profitability by retaining existing customers and attracting new ones.
- **Reduced costs:** A standards-based approach to information security ensures that all controls are measured and managed in a structured manner. This ensures that processes and procedures are more streamlined and effective, thus reducing costs. Some companies have found they can better manage the tools they have in place by consolidating redundant systems or

reassigning other systems from assets with low risk to those with higher risk.

- **Compliance with legislation:** Having a structured ISMS in place makes the task of compliance much easier.

- **Improved management:** Knowing what is in place and how it should be managed and secured makes it easier to manage information resources within a company.

- **Improved customer and partner relationships:** If a company demonstrates that it takes information security seriously, customers and trading partners can deal with it confidently, knowing that the company has taken an independently verifiable approach to information security risk management.

CHAPTER 4: IDENTIFY YOUR INFORMATION ASSETS

In order to know what protections and controls you should implement, it is important that you first understand what it is you are trying to protect. The standard expects that all information assets within the scope of the implementation of ISO27001 have been properly identified and a value placed on them.

So our first step in identifying our information assets should be to define the scope of the ISMS and identify what it will cover.

Define the scope of the ISMS

The scope is one of the most important items in planning your implementation of ISO27001. How broadly you define the scope will impact the amount of work and time required to roll out your ISO27001-based ISMS.

The scope of the ISMS could simply be described as the boundaries within which your ISMS applies. This could simply be a department within an organisation, a local office within an organisation or the whole organisation itself. Correctly defining the scope will have a direct relationship to the amount of effort required to implement an ISO27001-based ISMS within your organisation.

For this reason, some companies prefer to limit their initial implementation of the ISO27001 information security standard to an identifiably separate section within the organisation. Once this is successful, the scope is then expanded to gradually include other parts of the organisation. Other companies prefer to broach the project head on and will look to include the whole organisation within the scope from the outset. Their argument in favour of this approach is that information security is important to the whole organisation, or that the amount of effort required to include the whole organisation within the scope is not that much greater than that for restricting the scope to one area.

When deciding the scope for your own organisation, you should take items into account, such as:

- The size of your organisation and whether it is feasible to implement the standard within the whole organisation or just in certain sections;
- The number of different locations your organisation operates in and what legislation applies to each location;
- The commitment of senior management to the project – do you have their full support to implement the standard throughout the whole organisation?
- The extent of the documented policies, processes and procedures already in place;
- The number of staff who are already familiar with the ISO27001 information security standard;
- The timeline within which you wish to have the ISO27001 information security standard implemented.

Identifying your information security assets

Many people, when they think of assets, immediately think about hardware and other physical items, such as computers, printers, buildings and software. While these items are indeed important financial assets, you also need to identify all your information assets. Information assets are those assets that the business depends on to ensure the confidentiality, integrity and availability of its information. So a key information asset is the information itself that the organisation depends on, such as customer databases, staff files, intellectual property and, of course, the systems (those financial assets mentioned earlier), plus the people and services that ensure that information is secure.

I often recommend that people should look at their information assets in the groupings shown in Table 2.

Table 2: Information asset classification

Physical	Logical	Services
These include assets, such as: Buildings Computers Network equipment Furniture Electrical equipment Facilities management equipment, such as UPS, fire suppression, etc. People Software Paper records	Assets within this classification are typically those that relate to information, such as: Client database Documents Files Accounting data Payroll data Financial spreadsheets Reputation of the organisation Intellectual property Supplier contracts Software	Services that enable you to support your ISMS should be identified: Electricity supply Water supply HR expertise Recruitment firms ISPs Telecommunications provider Alarm monitoring services Physical security services IT equipment maintenance

It is important to remember that not all assets will fit neatly into just one category. For example, some information may be held in physical format as well as logical form. A contract could be held in physical format with the appropriate signatures on it while at the same time there may be electronic copies of the contract held on the systems. Each instance of the contract is a separate asset.

Information asset classification

Once you have identified your information assets, it is important that you specify how those assets should be treated in accordance with their value to the organisation. Something that is of high value or a sensitive nature should be treated differently to an information asset that does not hold the same value. For example, the employees' payroll file should be handled more securely than a press release that is now in the public domain.

This discipline is known as data classification and handling. The concept is that you group information assets into different classifications based on their value, their sensitivity, how critical they are to the organisation or a combination of any of the above. Anyone who watches spy movies will be familiar with this concept already as it is similar to marking information 'top secret', 'for your eyes only', etc. While these may not be the actual titles you use for your own organisation, the concept is pretty much the same. These classifications can then be used by people to know immediately how they should handle these information assets, who they can share the information with and how to put new information into the appropriate classification when they create it.

The value of information assets

Each of the assets should also have a value. This value could be monetary based, such as the cost of an information asset, or it could be based on the perceived value of the asset to your organisation. For example, the client database could be valued based on the cost of the software to support the database, the number of hours to compile the information and the costs of the hardware and equipment to host the database. Alternatively, the value could be based on how important your organisation thinks this information is to it from a business point of view; does it have a high, medium or low value?

Once you have identified the value of an information asset, it then makes it easier to decide on what controls need to be put in place to protect that asset. If the information asset is valued at, say, US$10,000 then it does not make sense to spend US$25,000 to protect it.

What information security controls and countermeasures you need to put in place will depend on your risk assessment. Your risk assessment will help identify what the most appropriate controls are based on the value and classification of the information asset.

CHAPTER 5: CONDUCTING A RISK ASSESSMENT

Effectively running and managing an ISMS requires the system to be based upon a solid risk assessment and subsequent risk management disciplines. This means you need to have a formal process in place to identify and rate the different types of information security risks that exist against your information assets in terms of their impact and the likelihood of occurrence.

Once you have identified all the appropriate information security management risks, you need to put in place a formal process to assess and manage those risks. It is important that this process is one that you can repeat at regular periods in order to re-evaluate the risks.

Before we conduct a risk assessment, we need to understand what we mean by risk. Unfortunately, trying to define risk within the information security arena can generate heated debates similar to those about what the best operating system is. There are many different opinions about risk and how best to manage it and this book will not delve into the intricacies of the topic. Instead, we will take a much broader view to enable you to understand risk at a high level, within the requirements of ISO27001, and provide you with the basis upon which you can further build that understanding.

According to ISO/IEC 27000:2012, risk is defined as the 'effect of uncertainty on objectives'. While this may not appear to be a straightforward definition, it essentially states that risks are those things that can interfere with or totally negate your organisation's objectives.

It should be noted that this definition allows the possibility that risk can have positive outcomes, such as a rise in a share price or gambling on a horse in a race, as well as negative ones. In the context of information security, however, it is more common to work on the basis that all risks have a negative outcome.

What is risk?

Before we can assess and manage the risks to the information assets you identified in the previous chapter, we need to understand what exactly it is we are trying to manage. Firstly, you should realise that risk is a definable event and therefore should be identified and managed. To better manage risks, our main concerns should be about how often the identified risk can happen and the impact of the risk should it happen. In its simplest form, risk can be shown as:

Risk = Likelihood (Vulnerability * Threat) * Impact

The purpose of implementing information security controls is to reduce either the likelihood of the risk happening or its impact. It is important to remember, however, that risk cannot be eliminated entirely and the purpose of your risk assessment and risk management programme is to identify the appropriate controls that will reduce the level of risk to an acceptable one.

To better understand risk, we need to spend some time understanding its different elements.

Vulnerability

According to the Risk Management Guide for Information Technology Systems, a vulnerability is:

[A] weakness in an information system, system security procedures, internal controls, or implementation that could be exploited by a threat source. [3]

In other words, a vulnerability is simply a condition that exists that could cause harm to your organisation should a threat take advantage of that condition. Therefore, having a vulnerability by itself may not cause any harm; it is a threat taking advantage of the vulnerability that causes harm to the information asset. Vulnerabilities are not confined to technical vulnerabilities, such as bugs in software, but can manifest themselves as holes or weaknesses in other elements of your ISMS, such as poor user training, flammable material left in a computer room, poor passwords or badly configured systems. Some other examples of vulnerabilities are:

- Absence of key personnel
- Unstable power grid
- Unprotected cabling
- Lack of security awareness
- Software bugs
- Poor passwords
- Out-of-date anti-virus software
- No firewall installed.

---

[3] *Guide for Conducting Risk Assessments*, National Institute of Standards and Technology, 2012, p.9. *http://csrc.nist.gov/publications/nistpubs/800-30-rev1/sp800_30_r1.pdf*.

Threats to information

As previously mentioned, vulnerabilities by themselves do not cause any problems; it is the exploitation of those vulnerabilities by a threat that causes concerns. The impact on your organisation together with the likelihood of a threat exploiting a vulnerability are what determine the level of risk posed.

A threat is an event or series of events that occurs and which, because of the existence of a vulnerability, results in an undesired impact on information security assets. Remember that without a relevant vulnerability, a threat cannot create risk for an organisation – but equally the failure or inability to identify a vulnerability does not mean that it does not exist.

As information is one of the most important assets that a company possesses, it is important that the threats to that asset are properly identified and understood. There are a number of different threats that can exploit vulnerabilities to undermine the confidentiality, integrity and/or availability of the information assets you are trying to protect. In the main, threats can be classified into three key categories:

- Human-based threats
- Natural threats
- Technological threats.

While the following threats do not constitute an exhaustive list, they should serve to highlight some of the main threat classes.

Theft

An information asset could be stolen. For example, a laptop could be stolen during a break-in to your office or a copy of your customer database could be taken by a disgruntled employee moving to a rival company.

Loss

Losing an information asset is something that is unfortunately too common. Information could be copied on to a USB key that subsequently goes missing, a back-up tape could be mislaid or a CD-ROM containing confidential company information could go missing in the post. Another common way that information is lost is by someone accidentally destroying a file by deleting it from the system or by placing it in a shredder.

Intrusion

The threat to information that most people are aware of is that of the external hacker breaking into computer systems. As we connect more and more of our computers and networks to the Internet, we expose ourselves more and more to the threat of an unauthorised external party gaining access to our systems and data.

Corruption

Another threat posed to information is that of corruption. This can be caused by either deliberate or accidental means. Deliberate corruption of our information can be caused by an individual intentionally altering the data, perhaps to facilitate or cover up fraudulent activity. Accidental corruption is a more common threat and one that can happen as a result of poor end-user or IT-administrator training, simple human error or technical issues, such as power outages, disk failures or system crashes.

Deliberate corruption is more sinister and often is the result of a disgruntled employee seeking revenge against their employer by maliciously altering data. Alternatively, deliberate corruption could be caused by an external party trying to gain advantage (e.g. altering the price of an item on an e-commerce website), the defacing of a website or as the result of industrial espionage.

Denial of service

Denial of service or access is another threat to information by undermining its availability. This could be in the form of a denial-of-service attack against an organisation's website by sending so much traffic to it that it cannot process the amount of requests it is receiving. Another type of denial-of-service attack is to prevent physical access to information by, for example, damaging locks to a filing room or cabinet.

Natural threats

Natural threats also need to be considered as threats against information. Fire is the threat that most people think of when we speak about this category of threat and indeed it can be the most destructive. However, there are other natural threats that we should not forget, such as water, either as a result of a flood or a leak in the plumbing of a building; dampness promoting fungal growth, which destroys paper-based records; and rodents, which can chew their way through electrical and network cables or destroy paper records.

All of the above are simply examples of the types of threat against your information assets that you must consider and there may be threats unique to your own particular business environment. What we will achieve over the coming chapters is to understand how the ISO27001 information security standard, together with Microsoft's technology, can be used to manage these threats.

Managing risks

Information security risks need to be managed on a formal basis and reviewed regularly to ensure that they are being managed in accordance with updates to the organisation's business practices and updates to, or adoption of new, technologies.

A risk register should be created and all identified risks recorded. A risk treatment plan should also be developed outlining what controls are already in place, what additional controls need to be implemented and details of who is responsible for implementing and managing those controls.

Once you have identified the risks, you then need to decide how best to manage those risks. There are a number of ways you can manage risks.

Risk acceptance

You may identify risks that exist against certain assets but you accept that there are no additional controls that you can put in to prevent the risk from occurring, or if the risk does occur, its impact has been reduced to a level that is acceptable to the business.

Of course, from time to time there may be risks that you can do nothing about but could still have a major impact on the business. In this case, the organisation may accept the risk and continue with it being at a certain level until it can be properly mitigated at a later date.

Risk mitigation

This is where you identify additional controls to either eliminate or reduce the identified risk and thereby reduce its probability of occurrence or its impact. These can be technical, procedural or physical controls.

Risk avoidance

There may be certain risks that your organisation feels are too great to manage and therefore the best course of action is to avoid them. For example, if a new IT project was going to undermine the security of the computer network, it might be cancelled as the risk posed to the organisation might outweigh the benefits the IT project would have brought.

Risk transfer

Some organisations may feel that they cannot manage certain risks by themselves and therefore engage with a third party to share or pass on that risk. Outsourcing certain functions would be seen as a risk transfer; however the most common form of risk transfer would be purchasing insurance against a certain risk materialising.

Risk deference

The deference of a risk is similar to risk avoidance except in this case the organisation does not decide to cancel an action or activity to avoid a certain risk but instead may postpone that activity to a later and more suitable date. For example, a project to enable e-commerce on a website may be postponed until the website's underlying technology is made more secure.

The different types of risk analysis

There are two main approaches to risk analysis: quantitative and qualitative. Both approaches have their pluses and minuses and, as with the risk management tools, which one to use is entirely up to you and the needs and culture of your organisation.

Quantitative risk analysis

With this approach the goal is to assign a value - be that monetary or otherwise - to an information security asset. For example, a common approach to use in this type of risk analysis is to assign a monetary value to all information assets whether those assets are tangible or intangible.

Once you have assigned a value to each information security asset, it becomes quite easy to identify those that have the most value to the organisation. Based on your analysis of the threats faced by the various information assets, you can quickly identify the potential loss for each risk.

This information can then be used to identify which information security assets you should concentrate on securing in order to minimise loss to the company. This approach can be quite useful when trying to justify investment in security controls as you can demonstrate the potential savings in loss prevention the control will bring. For example, if you have an asset worth €100,000 and an investment of €5,000 in a security control would prevent a potential €20,000 loss by reducing an identified risk, then the approval process for that investment is an easy argument to make.

The advantages of quantitative risk analysis

The following are the main benefits of employing a quantitative risk management methodology:

- It employs probability concepts which focus on the likelihood that a risk will or will not occur.
- The value of information is expressed in monetary terms with supporting rationale. This can be quite useful when justifying budgetary spend.
- The results of the risk assessment are expressed in terms and language that senior management understands.

The disadvantages of quantitative risk management

The following are some of the disadvantages of the qualitative risk management approach:

- A pure quantitative risk analysis methodology may not be possible because quantitative measures must be applied to some assets that may not have an intrinsic value attached to them. For example, what financial value should be placed on assets like the organisation's reputation?

- Since this methodology is based on specific values, the results can appear less ambiguous than the qualitative approach. However, be aware that using numbers can give an appearance of specificity that does not really exist.

- In order to effectively use this methodology, a large amount of data must be gathered, analysed and managed. This can add time, overheads and demands on resources to conducting the risk assessment.

Qualitative risk management

Qualitative risk management takes a more relative approach than quantitative risk management. Instead of assigning hard numeric values to information assets, the qualitative approach assigns more descriptive and relative values, such as 'high, medium or low'.[4]

With this approach, an organisation can quickly assess the level of risk against the various information assets based on opinions and feedback. The values are often based on subjective rather than objective data, however, which can mean that it may be difficult to ensure consistent results each time the process is done.

---

[4] For a thorough discussion of this subject, see *Information Security Risk Management for ISO27001*, 2nd edition, Calder A and Watkins S, ITGP (2010).

The advantages of qualitative risk management

The following are the main benefits of employing a qualitative risk management methodology:

- A qualitative risk management approach is often seen as the easiest and quickest way to conduct your risk management.
- It is simple and readily understood and executed as it does not rely on numbers and formulae to determine the levels of risk.
- It provides a general indication of significant areas of risk that should be addressed.

The disadvantages of qualitative risk management

The following are some of the main disadvantages of the qualitative risk management methodology:

- It can be difficult to enforce a uniform and consistent approach when identifying and assessing risks.
- This methodology is subjective in both its process and metrics.
- Unlike the quantitative risk management approach, the qualitative approach may not provide meaningful cost/benefit analysis.

The quantitative versus qualitative approach

Table 3, sourced from (ISC)²'s CISSP Common Body of Knowledge Review Seminar, demonstrates a particular view of the main differences between the two approaches.

Table 3: Comparison of quantitative and qualitative risk management

Quantitative	Attributes	Qualitative
Yes	Provides independent and objective metrics	No
Yes	Enables cost benefit analysis	No
Yes	Is monetary based	No
No	Takes the least amount of work and time	Yes
No	Requires the least amount of information	Yes
Yes	Can be easily automated	No
No	Requires a certain amount of guesswork	Yes
Yes	Results in the value of information being understood	No
Yes	Requires additional information, such as threat frequency and impact data	No

It should be noted that the $(ISC)^2$ view is not universally supported; there is a strongly articulated argument that qualitative risk assessment is clearer, more objective and more widely and easily understood; this argument is made most strongly in *Information Security Risk Management for ISO27001*[5].

Risk management tools

There are numerous risk management tools and methodologies available, ranging from commercial products to free or open source tools. You should also note that the ISO27001 information security standard does not specify which one you should use, but it does provide an outline of the process, which is aligned with ISO31000. Because your organisation is unique, the way your organisation deals with and treats risks will also be unique. Therefore, whatever tool or methodology you choose will be specific to your environment.

While the scope of this book does not allow for an in-depth analysis or discussion on the various methodologies that are available, the most commonly seen methodologies are described below.

OCTAVE (Operationally Critical Threat, Asset, and Vulnerability Evaluation) is a free methodology developed by Carnegie Mellon University, SEI (Software Engineering Institute) *www.cert.org/resilience/products-services/octave/*; you should note that it is possible to implement OCTAVE in a way that does not meet the requirements of ISO27001, and this is an issue that should be carefully explored by anyone looking to use OCTAVE.

NIST SP 800-30 Guide for Conducting Risk Assessments is a free methodology published by the United

---

[5] *Information Security Risk Management for ISO27001*, 2nd edition, Calder A and Watkins S, ITGP, 2010.

State's National Institute for Standards and Technology (NIST) *csrc.nist.gov/publications/PubsSPs.html*.

vsRisk is a specialist ISO27001 information security risk assessment tool developed by Vigilant Software and specifically designed to use a qualitative methodology; more information is available from *www.vigilantsoftware.co.uk*.

If you require more information on any of the above tools or indeed any of the other tools that are widely available, the European Network and Information Security Agency (ENISA) has published an online inventory of risk management and risk assessment tools on their website at *www.enisa.europa.eu/activities/risk-management/current-risk/risk-management-inventory*. This review provides an overview of the main methodologies that you can employ together with an overview of the available tools. The site also has an interesting comparison tool which will allow you to review and compare the tools against each other to determine which may be most suitable for you.

Microsoft Security Risk Management Guide[6]

Microsoft provides a free technology-agnostic guide on how to conduct information security risk management. The guide explains the basics of risk assessment and helps you to identify the various risks. The guide also provides a number of templates in Microsoft® Word and Microsoft® Excel® format to help you perform your risk analysis. We will discuss this guide in more detail later on in this book.

---

[6] *www.microsoft.com/en-us/download/details.aspx?id=6232*

5: Conducting a Risk Assessment

It is important to remember that you can also use your own risk assessment system. This could be a system that is already in place for other disciplines in your organisation, such as project management. There is no requirement to purchase any particular tool but whatever way you choose to manage your risks, you need to ensure that it is something that conforms to the requirements of ISO27001 in terms of the steps through which the risk assessment progresses, is easily understood, is repeatable and can be easily used to conduct regular risk assessments.

CHAPTER 6: AN OVERVIEW OF MICROSOFT TECHNOLOGIES

This chapter will provide an overview of the security features of the Microsoft technologies commonly found in most organisations. This book will provide you with enough information to understand the main security benefits provided by each technology, with useful implementation guidance. The technologies that we will focus on are:

- Microsoft® Windows Server® 2012
- Microsoft® Windows Server® 2008
- Microsoft® Windows® 8
- Microsoft® Windows® 7
- Microsoft® Forefront™
- Microsoft® Forefront™ Threat Management Gateway
- Microsoft® Systems Center
- Microsoft® Windows Server® Update Services
- Microsoft® Baseline Security Analyzer
- Microsoft Security Risk Management Guide
- Microsoft® Security Assessment Tool
- Microsoft® Threat Analysis and Modeling Enterprise Edition
- Microsoft® CAT.NET
- Microsoft® Source Code Analyzer for SQL Injection

We will now discuss the main security features of each of the above products, while later on in the book we will detail how to implement and configure some of these technologies in line with the controls outlined in ISO27001.

Microsoft® Windows Server® 2008

Microsoft® Windows Server® 2008[7] is one of Microsoft's latest operating systems and was developed as part of Microsoft's Trusted Computing Initiative. It is among the most secure operating systems ever developed by Microsoft. It has a number of built-in security features that will enable you to ensure your Microsoft-based IT infrastructure is compliant with your ISO27001 ISMS.

Security features of Microsoft® Windows Server® 2008

As well as the standard security features installed in earlier versions of Microsoft® Windows Server®, Microsoft® Windows Server® 2008 has a number of new features that vastly improve on its security:

- Read-only domain controller
- BitLocker™ drive encryption
- Server Core
- Network Access Protection
- Routing and Remote Access Service
- Windows® Firewall with advanced security
- Active Directory® Certificate Services
- Active Directory® Rights Management Services
- Group policies.

We will briefly look at each feature to see how it can benefit you when implementing your ISMS based on the ISO27001 information security standard.

---

[7] *www.microsoft.com/windowsserver2008/en/us/default.aspx.*

Read-only domain controller

Microsoft® Windows Server® 2008 introduces a new type of domain controller called a read-only domain controller (RODC). The RODC was designed for organisations which need to deploy a domain controller in a remote office to facilitate users logging on to the domain or to support some applications that are required to be run on a domain controller. The RODC provides all the functions and features of a normal domain controller except that it contains a read-only version of the Active Directory® Domain Services database which cannot be changed.

This allows an organisation to securely deploy a domain controller into a less physically secure environment, such as a remote office, with the confidence of knowing that no unauthorised changes can be made to the RODC.

BitLocker™ drive encryption

Windows BitLocker™ drive encryption[8] (BitLocker™) is a security feature that first appeared in Microsoft® Windows Vista® and now features as an optional component for Microsoft® Windows Server® 2008. You can use BitLocker™ in Microsoft® Windows Server® 2008 to protect volumes used for data storage.

Windows BitLocker™ can be used to encrypt all data stored on the Windows® operating system volume and any configured data volumes. When encrypting the operating system volume you will also encrypt the Windows Server® 2008 operating system, application files, system paging and

---

[8] *www.microsoft.com/windows/windows-vista/features/bitlocker.aspx.*

hibernation files and any data stored on the encrypted system or data volumes.

Server Core

Microsoft® Windows Server® 2008 provides you with the option to install a server with a minimal environment to help you improve security and reduce management of servers in a certain role. This type of installation is called a Server Core[9] installation option.

You can use a Server Core installation for Microsoft® Windows Server® 2008 to provide the following server roles:

- Active Directory® Domain Services
- Active Directory® Lightweight Directory Services (AD LDS)
- DHCP server
- DNS server
- File services
- Print server
- Internet Information Services 7.0
- Hyper-V.

A Server Core installation reduces your administrative effort and help limits the security risks as the server is running just the bare essentials to provide for its role and functionality.

The Server Core installation does not have a graphical user interface and any unnecessary services are not installed.

---

[9] *www.microsoft.com/windowsserver2008/en/us/compare-core-installation.aspx.*

This provides for a very streamlined server environment that can also be more secure than a normal server installation.

Network Access Protection

Microsoft introduced Network Access Protection[10] (NAP) with Windows Server® 2008. Network Access Protection is a technology to enable you to ensure that all devices are properly authenticated, have the appropriate levels of anti-virus software installed on them and that their software is patched to the appropriate level before they're allowed to connect to your organisations network. Should a computer try to connect to your network that does not comply with your policy, you can direct it to access limited resources in order to remedy the identified issue, such as outdated anti-virus software, before allowing full connection to the network.

Routing and Remote Access service

The Routing and Remote Access[11] service in Windows Server® 2008 enables you to provide remote users access to your organisation's private network over a virtual private network (VPN). With a server configured to support the Routing and Remote Access service you can also connect two networks over the Internet, such as a branch office to your head office, via a VPN.

---

[10] *http://technet.microsoft.com/en-us/network/bb545879.aspx.*
[11] *http://technet.microsoft.com/en-us/network/bb545655.aspx.*

You can also use the Routing and Remote Access service in conjunction with the Network Access Protection service to ensure that all remote users comply with your minimum security requirements.

Windows® Firewall with Advanced Security

The Windows® Firewall with Advanced Security[12] is the first firewall to be enabled by default on a Windows Server® operating system. Windows® Firewall with Advanced Security protects your server from any unauthorised traffic and enables you to better protect your information assets. By employing the Windows® Firewall with Advanced Security you can also use Internet Protocol security (IPsec) to create secure communications from one point on the network to another.

Active Directory® Certificate Services

Within Microsoft®'s Windows Server® 2008, the Active Directory® Certificate Services provide you with the ability to manage your own public key certificates to be used either to provide additional authentication to end-users or to support the enabling of secure traffic to an e-commerce website.

---

[12] *www.microsoft.com/downloads/details.aspx?FamilyID=DF192E1B-A92A-4075-9F69-C12B7C54B52B&displaylang=en.*

Active Directory® Rights Management Services

The Active Directory® Rights Management Services[13] within Microsoft® Windows Server® 2008 enable you to manage how documents are stored and transmitted within your organisation. With Active Directory® Rights Management Services you can configure your data to be managed in accordance with your data classification and handling policy. You can configure your system to encrypt data, restrict access to it and determine how it can be sent by email, depending on the classification of the file.

Group Policies

Group Policies are a powerful feature within Microsoft® Windows Server® 2008 that enables you to control the Windows® environment for all of your users. With Group Policies you can set up different policies for different types of users. For example, you could create a Group Policy to enforce a stringent password policy on all users within a certain user group, for example IT, with a different and less stringent password policy for normal users.

With Group Policies you can also, in line with your access policy, lock down the desktop for the end-users so that all they see are the applications that they require to do their business function.

You can also use a Group Policy in Windows Server® 2008 to prevent users from using removable storage devices on their computers, such as USB keys, MP3 players, portable hard disks and smartphones. This feature can help prevent

---

[13] *http://technet.microsoft.com/en-us/library/cc771307.aspx.*

the introduction of a virus into your network by preventing users from plugging an infected device into a PC or prevent the compromise or theft of information assets or personal data using these devices.

The above are just some of the features of Microsoft® Windows Server® 2008. There are many other features, parameters and configurations that you can employ to better protect your environment.

Microsoft® Windows Server® 2012

Microsoft® Windows Server® 2012[14] is one of Microsoft's latest operating systems and, like the previous version, was developed as part of Microsoft's Trusted Computing Initiative. It is among the most secure operating systems ever developed by Microsoft. It has a number of built-in security features that will enable you to ensure your Microsoft-based IT infrastructure is compliant with your ISO27001 ISMS.

Security features of Microsoft® Windows Server® 2012

Microsoft® Windows Server® 2012 includes the majority of the security features included in Microsoft® Windows Server® 2008, updated as appropriate. Many of the updates and advances take advantage of newer technologies and awareness of the current state of information and cyber security. As such, these features are generally more effective than those incorporated into Microsoft® Windows Server® 2008.

---

[14] *www.microsoft.com/windowsserver2008/en/us/default.aspx.*

In addition, there are some new features included in Microsoft® Windows Server® 2012 and Microsoft® Windows Server® 2012 R2:

- Dynamic Access Control
- Windows® PowerShell
- Failover clustering

Dynamic Access Control

Dynamic Access Control gives you data governance control over your file servers, making it simpler to control who has access to information and to audit access data. This is essentially an extension of group policies incorporating recognition of data classification. Policies can be constructed to ensure that all data is protected from unauthorised access, that all access is logged for ease of audit, and to apply automatic Rights Management Services (RMS) encryption.

Windows® PowerShell

Windows® PowerShell takes the Server Core feature from Microsoft® Windows Server® 2008 (which enables you to control the flexibility of a Windows® installation) and allows the administrator to switch the server core dynamically. This provides a greater degree of control and flexibility over the access a user has to systems, services and external facilities.

Failover clustering

Microsoft® Windows Server® 2012 allows the administrator to define a group of independent computer to work together to increase the availability and scalability of clustered applications and services. These clusters can thus be used to ensure that applications and services remain available when errors occur or during ICT continuity issues, such as a localised power failure.

Microsoft® Windows® 7

Microsoft® Windows® 7[15] is Microsoft's previous desktop operating system. It has many features that improve its security over earlier Microsoft operating systems. It is also based on the same core as Microsoft® Windows Server® 2008 and builds upon many of the security features first featured in Microsoft Windows Vista®. There are a number of security features within Microsoft® Windows® 7 that could be of interest to you when considering how to manage your ISO27001 ISMS:

- Windows® Backup and Restore Center
- BitLocker™
- DirectAccess
- AppLocker™
- Windows® Firewall
- Windows® Defender
- User Account Control
- Windows® Security Center.

---

[15] *www.microsoft.com/windows/windows-7/default.aspx.*

Microsoft® Windows® 8

Microsoft® Windows® 8[16] is Microsoft's latest desktop operating system. In addition to those features offered in Microsoft® Windows® 7, updated as appropriate, it includes several new features of interest to you when considering how to manage your ISO27001 ISMS:

- Windows To Go
- Microsoft® Secure Boot

Windows To Go

Windows To Go allows you to set up a bootable USB (or other mobile storage device) containing a corporate Windows® 8 environment. Windows To Go includes a number of security features, such as eliminating access to local hardware. In this way, the organisation could use the mobile storage device to present information to an external client or partner without exposing the corporate environment to threats present on the host's hardware. Furthermore, the Windows To Go drive can be encrypted using BitLocker™ for added security.

Windows® Backup and Restore Center

The Windows® Backup and Restore Center[17] within Microsoft® Windows® 7 and 8 offers you two ways to ensure that data stored on desktops or on laptops is backed up in order to protect it in the event of a failure of the computer, deletion or corruption of the data files or a

---

[16] *http://windows.microsoft.com/en-gb/windows-8/meet; currently in version 8.1.1.*
[17] *http://windows.microsoft.com/en-us/windows7/products/features/backup-and-restore*

problem with the operating system itself. These two options are:

- Automatic backup
- Complete backup

Automatic Backup

Automatic Backup allows you to configure your system to back up important files to a back-up location, be that a network share or an external hard drive attached to the computer. Automatic Backup will back up the data you specify in accordance with a schedule that you can set up. This results in your data being regularly backed up without any intervention from you.

Complete Backup

To guard against catastrophic failure of your system, Complete Backup enables you to take a back-up of the complete computer environment including the Windows® 7 operating system, system files, system settings, user settings, data and any installed programs.

BitLocker™

Windows® 7 and 8 still have the Encrypting File System that was introduced with Windows Vista®[18] and which allows you to encrypt individual files and folders. For example, if two users are sharing a computer, an

---

[18] *http://technet.microsoft.com/en-us/library/cc700811.aspx.*

administrator can use Encrypting File System to encrypt each user's data to make it unavailable to the other user. For network file and folder encryption, Windows® 7 enhances Encrypting File System management by enabling administrators to store Encrypting File System keys on smart cards.

Windows® 7 built on this data protection feature by introducing BitLocker™[19] and BitLocker To Go™. BitLocker™ enables you to encrypt the entire hard disk contents to make the data stored on it unavailable to unauthorised personnel.

Should you wish to transport information securely from one system to another using portable devices, such as a USB key, BitLocker To Go™ provides you with that capability. BitLocker To Go™ can be configured to require encryption for any removable device that users may write to while also allowing unprotected portable devices to be accessed in read only mode. This ensures that data can only be transferred on portable devices in encrypted mode. Administrators can manage how BitLocker To Go™ is configured by determining the strength of the passphrase to be used, where the keys are stored for escrow purposes, if smart cards need to be used, or whether domain user credentials are required.

DirectAccess

A major challenge for many modern work environments is enabling a mobile workforce while at the same time ensuring secure access to corporate information assets for

---

[19] *http://windows.microsoft.com/en-us/windows7/products/features/bitlocker*

remote users. DirectAccess is built upon industry standards, such as IPsec and IPv6 to provide remote users with a secure remote access to the network without the need to install additional Virtual Private Network (VPN) software. Network administrators can control which assets remote users have access to. DirectAccess also provides the network administrator with the ability to manage those remote machines to ensure that they comply with the Domain Policy settings and also update software with required patches.

AppLocker™

One of the challenges faced by many organisations is to ensure that end users only use the applications that they need to do their job. However, traditional PC environments result in users having numerous applications available on their desktops; many of these applications may not be necessary and in some cases could pose a security risk if they are abused or misused. AppLocker™ allows an organisation to ensure only the applications a user requires to do their job are available on their desktop. This enables the organisation to ensure its systems are more secure, are compliant with its software licences, and that there is no unauthorised software running on their systems.

Windows® Firewall

Microsoft® Windows® 7 and 8 have their own personal software firewall and filters both outgoing and incoming traffic and blocks potentially malicious activity.

Windows® Firewall also has the IPsec protocol integrated into it by default. IPsec can be configured for securing connections over public networks to create VPNs. It can also be deployed internally in a network to ensure secure access to sensitive servers.

The Windows® Firewall within Microsoft® Windows® 7 and 8 has a feature called network awareness built into it. Network awareness enables you to create rules that are applied depending on the location of the computer. For example, the firewall can be configured to have a certain set of rules if the client connects to a wireless hotspot and a different set of rules if the client is connecting to your organisation's network.

Windows® Defender

Windows® Defender[20] is a program that is provided free as a download for Microsoft® Windows® XP and is included in Windows® 7. Windows® Defender runs constantly in the background to detect and protect against security threats caused by malware, such as spyware, keyloggers, adware programs and so on. Windows® Defender is automatically updated by Microsoft to protect against new threats.

Note that while Windows® Defender protects against spyware and other similar security threats, it is not a replacement for traditional anti-virus software. To maintain protection against all malicious software you should also ensure that effective third-party anti-virus software is installed on your Windows® 7 system to complement Windows® Defender.

---

[20] *http://windows.microsoft.com/en-us/windows7/products/features/windows-defender*

Windows® Defender for Microsoft® Windows® 8, however, has been updated to a true anti-virus program. This is comparable to Microsoft® Security Essentials, and uses the same virus definition updates. As such, Microsoft® Security Essentials is not compatible with Windows® 8.

User Account Control

User Account Control[21] (UAC) is a feature in Microsoft® Windows® 7 and 8 to segregate tasks that require administrator access from those of a standard user.

If a user is logged on with a standard user account and needs to perform a task that requires administrator privileges, Microsoft® Windows® 7 and 8 will prompt them for the appropriate administrator credentials to perform the task.

Windows® Security Center

In Microsoft® Windows® 7 and 8, the Windows® Security Center is a background process that constantly monitors the status of the key security components of the operating system, such as:

- Malware protection
- Other security settings

Windows® Security Center will prompt the user should it detect an issue with any of the above. For example, the malware protection component of Windows® Security Center will prompt the user should it identify that no

---

[21] *http://technet.microsoft.com/en-us/library/cc731416%28WS.10%29.aspx.*

malware protection software is installed and will also provide a link to various vendors. Should anti-malware software be installed and be out of date, the Windows® Security Center will prompt the user and provide them with a link to the relevant vendor to update the software.

Windows® Security Center will also monitor and advise the user on the security settings of Internet Explorer® and User Account Control.

In Windows® 8, Windows® Security Center monitors more items, providing a broader level of coverage.

Microsoft® Forefront™

Microsoft® Forefront™[22] is a suite of products to enable you to defend your network against a range of security threats, such as computer viruses, spam emails, rootkits and malicious network attacks. The Microsoft® Forefront™ suite of products includes the following components:

- **Microsoft® Forefront™ Threat Management Gateway:** Microsoft® Forefront™ Threat Management Gateway is a powerful application-type firewall that can protect your network from malicious external network traffic. It gives you granular control over the access that users have to Internet services and sites based on their user ID. It also supports running VPNs to securely connect remote users and offices to your core network infrastructure.
- **Microsoft® Antigen:** With the Antigen[23] range of products Microsoft can provide you with the ability to

---

[22] *www.microsoft.com/forefront/threat-management-gateway/en/us/overview.aspx.*
[23] *http://technet.microsoft.com/en-us/library/bb913985.aspx*

use a combination of anti-virus scan engines developed by various third-party security companies and also by Microsoft to protect your server infrastructure from malicious code. You can deploy Microsoft® Antigen to provide server-level anti-virus, anti-spam, and content-filtering protection for services, such as Microsoft® Exchange Server, Microsoft® Office® Communicator and Microsoft® SharePoint® Services.

- **Microsoft® Forefront™ Client Security:** Microsoft® Forefront™ Client Security can protect your workstations, laptops and servers from various threats posed by malicious software, such as computer viruses, Trojans, spyware and keyloggers. With Microsoft® Forefront™ security you can centrally manage how your workstations are updated with new anti-virus signature files and updated software. It comes with a powerful reporting utility to allow you to detect when updates have failed, when a virus has been detected and what systems have out-of-date policies.

Microsoft® Systems Center

Microsoft® Systems Center[24] is a range of tools and products that you can use to better manage your IT infrastructure. Which products suit you will be based on your organisation's individual requirements. The key products are as follows.

- **Microsoft® Systems Center Configuration Manager:** Microsoft® Systems Center Configuration Manager provides you with the ability to manage and deploy your

---

[24] *www.microsoft.com/systemcenter/en/us/default.aspx*

servers and client PCs. You can centrally distribute and update your systems with updated applications or configuration changes, ensure that all systems are configured in line with your corporate policies and identify what software and hardware assets you have on your network.

- **Microsoft® Systems Center Operations Manager:** Microsoft® Systems Center Operations Manager provides you with the ability to constantly monitor your network to ensure it is running in a secure and optimised fashion. Microsoft® Systems Center Operations Manager will monitor key components of your network and alert you should events occur that could jeopardise the security or availability of your systems.

- **Microsoft® Systems Center Data Protection Manager:** The Microsoft® Systems Center Data Protection Manager provides you with a platform to centrally manage and control all your back-up, data protection and recovery services.

- **Microsoft® Systems Center Essentials:** If your organisation is of a medium size (say 500 PCs and 30 servers or fewer), Microsoft® System Center Essentials can provide you with a wide range of features to manage and secure your IT infrastructure. Microsoft® System Center Essentials provides you with the ability to monitor your servers, applications and PCs for critical events, facilitates hardware and software inventory and also provides software distribution and updates facilities.

Microsoft® Windows Server® Update Services

Managing software patches and updates to computers throughout an organisation can be a challenging.

Some companies use the approach of enabling each Microsoft® Windows® machine to automatically update itself when a new patch is released by Microsoft by using the Windows® Update Service built into the operating systems. However, this approach can prove problematic in that you have no control over how these patches are installed; nor are you able to manage the impact on your network bandwidth should many or all of the workstations start to update at the same time.

Best practice dictates that all patches should be thoroughly tested before being released and installed on production machines. Once a patch has been tested and approved, the actual distribution of it can be a challenge. If you have to physically visit each individual machine and manually update it, this could prove to be an expensive and time-consuming approach.

Microsoft® Windows Server® Update Services is a free tool from Microsoft that addresses this problem by allowing you to control how those updates are managed. With Microsoft® Windows Server® Update Services you install a centralised server on your network to manage the distribution of all patches. This allows you to download a patch, test it to ensure it has no adverse impacts on your environment and then push the patch out to all the client machines on your network. Microsoft® Windows Server® Update Services provides you with tools and utilities to monitor how effective the patch process has been, such as highlighting PCs that the patch did not apply to successfully.

Microsoft® Baseline Security Analyzer

Microsoft® Baseline Security Analyzer (MBSA) is a free tool from Microsoft that enables you to scan your network and detect computers that have missing patches for Microsoft's applications and operating systems that could be used by attackers or computer viruses to compromise those machines. Should the Microsoft® Baseline Security Analyzer detect that there are system misconfigurations or patches missing, it will present you with remediation advice on how best to resolve the problems.

Microsoft Security Risk Management Guide

Identifying, assessing and managing your information security risks are some of the critical steps to successfully implementing an ISMS based on the ISO27001 information security standard. Many people find this part of the process to be the most daunting, however, and one that is often improperly conducted. The main problem that many people have found is trying to figure out where to start. To help with this, Microsoft has developed their Microsoft Security Risk Management Guide[25]. The guide is available free and comes in a number of parts.

Firstly, it takes you through the whole risk management process in a step-by-step guide. Although written by Microsoft, the guide is not technology specific and indeed can be equally used to identify risks on other technology platforms.

---

[25] *www.microsoft.com/en-gb/download/details.aspx?id=6232*

The second part to the guide includes a series of templates to help you identify your information assets and assess the risks against them, and also includes a sample project plan that you can use.

Finally, the Microsoft Security Risk Management Guide includes a number of sample threats, vulnerabilities and information assets to help you start your risk management programme.

Microsoft® Threat Analysis and Modeling

Threat modelling is an important stage in the software development life cycle. This stage should be used to identify all of the threats that an attacker could use to exploit weaknesses or vulnerabilities in the application being developed. Without proper threat analysis and modelling for new applications, many organisations face the likelihood that security holes will be inherent in the application that at some point in the future could be exploited.

Microsoft® Threat Analysis and Modeling (TAM)[26] is another tool developed by the Microsoft ACE team. This tool allows non-technical people to build a threat model for a new application before it is developed. The threat model is based on the user roles, system components and data which are analysed by the TAM tool which by using a library of known attack types will report on what the potential threats within the application are. The TAM tool will also examine each of the identified threats and vulnerabilities and automatically analyse and generate a

---

[26] *www.microsoft.com/en-us/download/details.aspx?id=14719*

risk model, prioritising the items with potentially the highest risk that should be dealt with first. The tool will then generate a list of suggested steps that the developers should follow in order to minimise the identified risks.

Microsoft® CAT.NET

The Microsoft® Code Analysis Tool[27], Microsoft® CAT.NET, is a tool that enables you to scan your applications' source code to detect common security vulnerabilities. It is an automated tool and can be used on code developed in any of the .NET languages, such as .Net, C++®.NET, Visual Basic or C#™. The Microsoft® CAT.NET tool will examine your code for common coding mistakes that could lead to vulnerabilities, such as:

- Cross-site scripting (XSS)
- SQL injection
- Incorrect exception handling
- Process command injection
- Canonicalisation issues
- LDAP injection
- XPATH injection
- Redirection to user-controlled websites

Microsoft® CAT.NET uses a comprehensive library of known security issues found in source code that you can use to test your own source code. You also have the ability to amend or update the library with your own identified vulnerabilities. The tool scans each line of your source code

---

[27] *http://support.microsoft.com/kb/954476.*

and when a problem is detected, it will alert you to the issue with some guidelines on how to address the problem.

Microsoft® Source Code Analyzer for SQL Injection

As we continue to strengthen our network defences, attackers are moving more and more to attack our Web-based applications, in particular those that have interactive web pages which interface with a back-end database. One of the most common types of attack used is an SQL injection attack. This attack happens when a poorly written program allows user-provided data to be entered into a back-end database without any proper validation. This lack of validation enables an attacker to send database commands directly into the database to retrieve, delete or modify the data. The Microsoft® Source Code Analyzer for SQL Injection is another free security tool from Microsoft that allows your developers to scan their ASP source code to detect if there are any SQL Injection vulnerabilities in the code.

CHAPTER 7: IMPLEMENTING ISO27001 IN A MICROSOFT ENVIRONMENT

This section of this book will highlight how the various Microsoft technologies discussed previously can be deployed to implement controls selected as part of an ISMS based on the ISO27001 information security standard.

As discussed earlier in this book, the ISO27001 information security standard does not focus solely on technology and therefore there are a number of controls that will not use Microsoft technology solutions. Where possible, however, we will try to identify how the Microsoft solutions can support the implementation or ongoing management of such controls.

The following are extracts from the ISO27001 standard.

Section 4 Information security management system

Table 4: General requirements

ISO clause/control	Ref	Explanation	Controls
Information security management system	4.4	The organisation shall establish, implement, maintain and continually improve an ISMS, in accordance with the requirements of ISO27001.	A documented ISMS can be set up using Microsoft® IIS server to share and operate the ISMS.

Table 5: Operating the ISMS

ISO clause/control	Ref	Explanation	Controls
Operational planning and control	8.1	The organisation shall plan, implement and control the processes necessary to meet information security requirements. The organisation will define a risk assessment	Use Microsoft® IIS server to create and manage the ISMS. Use the Microsoft Security Risk Management Guide. Employ Microsoft® Security Assessment Tool.

		approach, and implement the risk assessment.	
Information security risk assessment	8.2	The organisation shall perform information security risk assessment at planned intervals or when significant changes are proposed or occur. The organisation shall retain documented information of the results of the information security risk assessments.	Use Microsoft® IIS server to create and manage the ISMS. Use the Microsoft Security Risk Management Guide. Use the Microsoft® Security Assessment Tool to assess your current security.
Information security risk treatment	8.3	The organisation shall implement the information security risk treatment plan. The	Use Microsoft® IIS server to create and manage the ISMS. Use the Microsoft Security Risk Management

		organisation shall retain documented information of the results of the information security risk treatment.	Guide. Use the Microsoft® Security Assessment Tool.
Management review	9.3	Top management shall review the organisation's ISMS at planned intervals to ensure its continuing suitability, adequacy and effectiveness. The outputs of the management review shall include decisions related to continual improvement opportunities and any needs for changes to the ISMS. The	Microsoft® IIS server can be used to share and communicate the regular findings of the ISMS reviews. Use the Microsoft® Security Assessment Tool to continuously review your security.

| | | organisation shall retain documented information of the results of management reviews. | |

Table 6: Documentation requirements

ISO clause/control	Ref	Explanation	Controls
Documented information - General	7.5.1	The organisation's ISMS shall include documented information required by ISO27001, and documented information necessary for the effectiveness of the ISMS.	A documented ISMS can be set up using Microsoft® IIS server to share and operate the ISMS. Templates can be set up in Microsoft® Word for documents, such as minutes, policies and procedures.
Documented information – Creating and updating	7.5.2	The organisation shall ensure that all documented information is appropriately identified and described; in an appropriate	Windows Server® Active Directory® Rights Management Services can be employed to ensure documents are controlled in

		format and media; and reviewed and approved for suitability and adequacy.	accordance with the policy. Documents can be stored securely within network shares and folders with the appropriate permissions for viewing, editing, creating and deleting.
Documented information – Control of documented information	7.5.3	Documented information required by the ISMS and by ISO27001 shall be controlled. Documented information of external origin shall be identified as appropriate and controlled.	Windows Server® Active Directory® Rights Management Services can be employed to ensure documents are controlled in accordance with the policy. Documents can be stored securely within network shares and folders with the appropriate permissions for viewing, editing, creating and deleting.

Table 7: A.5.1 Management direction for information security

ISO clause/control	Ref	Explanation	Controls
Policies for information security	A.5.1.1	A set of policies for information security shall be defined, approved by management, published and communicated to all appropriate employees and external parties.	The policy can be shared and displayed using Microsoft® IIS server.
Review of the policies for information security	A.5.1.2	The policies should be reviewed at planned intervals or when significant changes occur to ensure they remain auditable, adequate and effective.	The policy can be shared and displayed using Microsoft® IIS server.

Section A.6 Organisation of information security

Table 8: A.6.1 Internal organisation

ISO clause/control	Ref	Explanation	Controls
Information security roles and responsibilities	A.6.1.1	All information security roles and responsibilities are defined and allocated.	An organisational chart with the appropriate roles and responsibilities could be implemented on IIS server.
Segregation of duties	A.6.1.2	Conflicting duties and areas of responsibility shall be segregated to reduce opportunities for unauthorised or unintentional modification or misuse of organisational assets.	Ensure that users are in the most appropriate groups for their job roles. Avoid providing users with access to the administrator account or making their user IDs part of the administrator group. If users need to conduct tasks above the normal

			security requirements, ensure they have two accounts, one for their normal day-to-day tasks and the other for their elevated role. Enable auditing to track the activity of users on the systems.
Contact with authorities	A.6.1.3	Appropriate contacts should be maintained with the relevant authorities.	A page could be created within IIS to list all the appropriate contacts with the appropriate permissions for viewing.
Contact with special interest groups	A.6.1.4	Appropriate contacts should be maintained with relevant special interest groups or other specialist	A page could be created within IIS to list all the appropriate contacts with the appropriate permissions for viewing.

		security forums and professional associations	
Information security in project management	A.6.1.5	Information security should be addressed in project management, regardless of the type of project.	A page could be created within IIS to describe the procedure for incorporating information security in project planning and workflows. CAT.NET can be incorporated into software development projects to minimise the risk of insecure coding.

Table 9: A.6.2 Mobile devices and teleworking

ISO clause/control	Ref	Explanation	Controls
Mobile device policy	A.6.2.1	A policy and supporting security measures should be adopted to manage the risks	The policy can be shared and displayed using Microsoft® IIS server. Windows To

		introduced by using mobile devices.	Go can be used to minimise logical contact with external hardware.
			Install Microsoft® Forefront™ Antivirus on all mobile computers.
			Ensure Microsoft® Defender is running on all machines.
			Ensure that all systems have the latest patches by either using the Windows® Update Service or centrally managing all updates using Windows® System Update Service.
			Restricting user access rights to only what they require and not providing

			elevated privileges can prevent malicious software infecting a machine.
			Ensure that the firewall built into Windows® 7/8 is turned on and configured correctly.
			Deploy Microsoft® Forefront™ Threat Management Gateway at the network perimeter to control access to the network and force mobile users to use a VPN to access the network.
			Use BitLocker™ to encrypt sensitive data on the mobile devices.

			Regularly scan all systems for vulnerabilities using Microsoft® Baseline Security Analyzer. Deploy Microsoft® Network Access Protection to ensure only devices with the appropriate patch levels, anti-virus software and security configurations can access your network.
Teleworking	A.6.2.2	A policy and supporting security measures should be implemented to protect information accessed, processed or stored at teleworking sites.	The policy can be shared and displayed using Microsoft® IIS server. Deploy Microsoft® Network Access Protection to ensure only

			devices with the appropriate patch levels, anti-virus software and security configurations can access your network, especially if a remote user is using their own computer to connect to your network.
			Use DirectAccess to provide secure access for remote users.
			Use Dynamic Access Control to define appropriate teleworker user groups and control their access rights according to data governance principles.
			Use AppLocker™

			to provide access to restrict users to the applications they need for their job role.

Section A.7 Human resource security

Table 10: A.7.1 Prior to employment

ISO clause/control	Ref	Explanation	Controls
Screening	A.8.1.2	Verification checks on all staff will be carried out at the time of job applications.	Create workflow in IIS to ensure steps are completed.
Terms and conditions of employment	A.8.1.3	Contractual agreements with employees and contractors should state their and the organisation's responsibilities for information security.	Ensure that all relevant policies, which should include roles and responsibilities, are published on the IIS server. Publish a copy of the standard contract of employment on the IIS server.

Table 11: A.7.2 During employment

ISO clause/control	Ref	Explanation	Controls
Management responsibilities	A.7.2.1	Management should require employees and contractors to apply information security in accordance with the policies and procedures of the organisation.	All roles and responsibilities should be clearly documented and communicated to all staff either using IIS server or on a secure network share.
Information security education and training	A.7.2.2	All employees and contractors should receive appropriate awareness education and training, and regular updates in organisational policies and procedures.	A staff training matrix can be maintained in a Microsoft® Excel spreadsheet to record all relevant training. The IIS server can be used to publish regular security awareness messages to staff so that they are kept up to date with

| Disciplinary Process | A.7.2.3 | There should be a formal, communicated disciplinary process to take action against employees who commit an information security breach. | the latest threats and updates to any relevant policies.

You could publish the consequences of breaching the security policies either via the IIS server built into Windows Server® or on a shared network resource. |

Table 12: A.7.3 Termination and change of employment

ISO clause/control	Ref	Explanation	Controls
Termination or change of employment responsibilities	A.7.3.1	Information security responsibilities and duties that remain valid after termination or change of employment should be defined,	Use User Account Manager to ensure that all accounts are modified, disabled or deleted upon notification that the employee's

		communicate d and enforced.	contract of employment has been terminated or changed.

Section A.8 Asset management

Table 13: A.8.1 Responsibility for assets

ISO clause/control	Ref	Explanation	Controls
Inventory of assets	A.8.1.1	Assets associated with information and information processing facilities should be identified and inventoried.	Use the Microsoft Security Risk Management Guide. Use the Microsoft® Security Assessment Tool. Use Microsoft® Systems Center to identify all computer assets on the network.
Ownership of assets	A.8.1.2	Assets in the inventory should be owned.	Use the Microsoft Security Risk Management Guide.

Acceptable use of assets	A.8.1.3	Rules for the acceptable use of assets shall be identified, documented and implemented	All policies for the use of assets can be published and maintained on the IIS server.
Return of assets	A.8.1.4	All employees should return all of the organisation's assets in their possession upon termination of employment, contract or agreement.	Employ Active Directory® Rights Management Services to ensure any electronic copies of information assets are securely removed or erased from exiting employees' systems.

Table 14: A.8.2 Information classification

ISO clause/control	Ref	Explanation	Controls
Classification of information	A.8.2.1	Information should be classified according to legal requirements, value, criticality	Create templates in Microsoft® Office® products to automatically label documents

		and sensitivity to unauthorised disclosure or modification.	according to their classification.
			Employ Active Directory® Rights Management Services to ensure only authorised copies of the document are available.
			Store all documentation in secure locations on a Windows Server® 2008 share and set up the appropriate permissions.
			Connect classifications to Dynamic Access Control to ensure consistency across all users and information.
Labelling of information	A.8.2.2	The organisation should	Create templates in

		develop and implement an appropriate set of procedures for information labelling, in accordance with the information classification scheme.	Microsoft® Office® products to automatically label documents according to their classification. Employ the Active Directory® Rights Management Services to ensure only authorised copies of the document are available and that they are published and shared in accordance with the policy.
Handling of assets	A.8.2.3	The organisation should develop and implement procedures for handling assets, in accordance with the	Create templates in Microsoft® Office® products to automatically label documents according to

		information classification scheme.	their classification. Employ the Active Directory® Rights Management Services to ensure only authorised copies of the document are available and that they are published and shared in accordance with the policy. Connect classifications to Dynamic Access Control to ensure consistency across all users and information.

Table 15: A.8.3 Media handling

ISO clause/control	Ref	Explanation	Controls
Management of removable media	A.8.3.1	The organisation should develop and implement	Windows To Go can be used to minimise

| | | procedures for the management of removable media, in accordance with the information classification scheme. | logical contact with external hardware. Ensure that all sensitive data is encrypted using either BitLocker™ or BitLockerTo Go™. Use Group Policies to prevent users from using unauthorised USB devices, such as USB keys, MP3 players, external hard disks and smartphones. |
| Disposal of media | A.8.3.2 | All media will be disposed of in a secure manner when no longer required. | Ensure that all sensitive data is encrypted using either BitLocker™ or BitLockerTo Go™. Use Active Directory® Rights |

			Management Services to manage the handling of sensitive data.
			Windows To Go can be used to minimise logical contact with external hardware.
Physical media transfer	A.8.3.3	Media containing information will be protected from unauthorised access, misuse or corruption during transportation.	Ensure that all media being transported is encrypted by using BitLocker To Go™. Use Active Directory® Rights Management Services to manage the handling of sensitive data.

Section A.9 Access control

Table 16: A.9.1 Business requirements of access control

ISO clause/control	Ref	Explanation	Controls
Access control policy	A.9.1.1	An access control policy shall be established, documented and reviewed based on business and information security requirements.	Role-based access control can be set up in accordance with the business requirements. Regularly review the user accounts database to ensure that users are in appropriate groups with the relevant permissions for their current role and that accounts for staff no longer working for the organisation have been removed. Connect classifications to Dynamic

			Access Control to ensure consistency across all users and information.
Access to networks and network services	A.9.1.2	Users will only have access to networks and network services that they have been specifically authorised to use.	Regularly review user access and privileges to ensure users do not have excessive rights or access beyond what they should have. Ensure that servers are configured as outlined in Chapter 8 to prevent guest access or anonymous access to certain resources, such as named pipes. Connect classifications to Dynamic Access Control to ensure

			consistency across all users and information.

Table 17: A.9.2 User access management

ISO clause/control	Ref	Explanation	Controls
User registration	A.9.2.1	A formal registration and deregistration process will be implemented to enable assignment of access rights.	All users should have a unique user ID to identify themselves to the network. Regularly review the user accounts database to ensure that users are in appropriate groups with the relevant permissions for their current role and that accounts for staff no longer working for the organisation have been removed.
Privilege management	A.9.2.2	A formal user	Regularly

| | | access provisioning process should be implemented to assign or revoke access rights for all user types to all systems and services. | review the user accounts database to ensure that users are in appropriate groups with the relevant permissions for their current role and that accounts for staff no longer working for the organisation have been removed. Users requiring system privileges outside their normal user-level access should have a second account set up with those privileges so that the user has to log on |

			separately to use those privileges. This can prevent accidental corruption of systems by a user employing an account with too many privileges and also prevents the propagation of malicious code. Also activity using the privileged account can be monitored and audited.
			Connect classifications to Dynamic Access Control to ensure consistency across all users and information.

User password management	A.9.2.3	Allocation and use of privileged access rights should be restricted and controlled.	Use Group Policies to enforce strong passwords as outlined in Chapter 8.
Management of secret authentication information of users	A.9.2.4	Allocation of secret authentication information should be controlled through a formal management process.	Use Group Policies to enforce strong passwords as outlined in Chapter 8.
Review of user access rights	A.9.2.5	Asset owners should review users' access rights at regular intervals.	Regularly review the user accounts database to ensure that users are in appropriate groups with the relevant permissions for their current role and that accounts for staff no longer working for the organisation

			have been removed.
Removal of access rights	A.9.2.6	The access rights of all employees and external party users to information and information processing facilities should be removed upon termination of their employment, contract or agreement, or adjusted upon change.	Use User Account Manager to ensure that all accounts are disabled or deleted upon notification that the employee's contract of employment has been terminated, or adjusted when the employee's contract changes. Manage incremental access changes through Dynamic Access Control.

Table 18: A.9.3 User responsibilities

ISO clause/control	Ref	Explanation	Controls
Use of secret authentication information	A.9.3.1	All users will be required to follow the organisation's practices in the use of secret authentication information.	Use Group Policies to enforce strong passwords as outlined in Chapter 8.

Table 19: A.9.4 System and application access control

ISO clause/control	Ref	Explanation	Controls
Information access restriction	A.9.4.1	Access to information and application system functions should be restricted in accordance with the access control policy.	Regularly review the user accounts database to ensure that users are in appropriate groups with the relevant permissions for their current role and that accounts for staff no longer working for the organisation have been removed.

				For secure sites, consider using Group Policies to lock down the users' desktop to provide them with access only to the applications they need to perform their job.
				Windows® Terminal Services could be used to provide access to applications.
				Use AppLocker™ to provide access to restrict users to the applications they need for their job role.
				Connect classifications to Dynamic Access Control to ensure consistency

			across user groups and information.
Secure logon procedures	A.9.4.2	Access to systems and applications shall be controlled by a secure log-on procedure where required by the access control policy.	Ensure that the domain forces all users to log on using a unique user ID and password. For high-security sites consider using smart cards or biometrics for additional security.
Password management system	A.9.4.3	Password management systems should be interactive and ensure quality passwords.	Ensure that all systems and users comply with the domain password policy and that it is in force at all times. Chapter 8 outlines some suggested settings for the password management system.
Use of privileged	A.9.4.4	The use of utility programs that might be capable	System utility programs and other sensitive applications

| utility programs | | of overriding system and application controls should be restricted and tightly controlled. | should be configured to have their access restricted to only authorised users. Windows® file permissions could be used for this purpose. Alternatively you could consider using either EFS or BitLocker™ to encrypt the folders or volumes where these tools are located. Ensuring users do not have local administrator access to their PC will also help protect from users installing these programs on to their computer. |
| Access control to program | A.9.4.5 | Access to program source | Source code files can be |

source code		code should be restricted.	stored on secure shares with the appropriate permissions set so that only authorised personnel can access the code.
			Alternatively, Microsoft has a source code control solution available called Microsoft® Team Foundation Server.28 Team Foundation Server provides a database environment for managing control over source code. It also has features, such as data

---

28 More details are available at *http://msdn.microsoft.com/en-us/library/ms364061.aspx*.

			collection, reporting and project tracking. Microsoft® Team Foundation Server is part of the Visual Studio® Team System or it can be purchased separately.

Section A.10 Cryptography

Table 20: A.10.1 Cryptographic controls

ISO clause/control	Ref	Explanation	Controls
Policy on the use of cryptographic controls	A.10.1. 1	A policy on the use of cryptographic controls for protection of information should be developed and implemented.	The use of BitLocker™ and BitLocker To Go™ should comply with the policy as a result of the risk assessment. The use of FIPS-compliant algorithms for encryption, hashing and

			signing within Windows Server® 2008 can be configured through a registry setting, as outlined in Chapter 8.
Key management	A.10.1.2	A policy on the use, protection and lifetime of cryptographic keys should be developed and implemented through their whole lifecycle.	Windows Server® 2008 supports key management using Active Directory® Services.

Section A.11 Physical and environmental security

Table 21: A.11.1 Secure areas

ISO clause/control	Ref	Explanation	Controls
Physical security perimeter	A.11.1.1	Security perimeters should be defined and used to protect areas that contain either sensitive or critical	For servers and/or workstations located in secure areas, you could employ smart-card technology or

		information and information processing facilities.	biometrics as a means of authentication for users logging on to the systems. Deploy read-only domain controllers in remote offices or insecure locations. Use BitLocker™ to encrypt sensitive information held on servers and workstations.
Physical entry controls	A.11.1.2	Secure areas should be protected by appropriate entry controls to ensure that only authorised personnel are allowed access.	For servers and/or workstations located in secure areas, you could employ smart-card technology or biometrics as a means of authentication for users logging on to the systems.

Securing offices, rooms and facilities	A.11.1.3	Physical security for offices, rooms and facilities should be designed and applied.	Deploy read-only domain controllers in remote offices or insecure locations. Use BitLocker™ to encrypt sensitive information held on servers and workstations.
Protecting against external and environmental threats	A.11.1.4	Physical protection against natural disasters, malicious attack or accidents should be designed and applied.	You could employ Microsoft® System Center to monitor key environmental components of servers, such as temperature, etc. to ensure they are protected against environmental risks.
Working in secure areas	A.11.1.5	Procedures for working in secure areas should be designed and applied.	For servers and/or workstations located in secure areas, you could employ smart-

			card technology or biometrics as a means of authentication for users logging on to the systems.
			Deploy read-only domain controllers in remote offices or insecure locations.
			Use BitLocker™ to encrypt sensitive information held on servers and workstations.
Delivery and loading areas	A.11.1. 6	Access points such as delivery and loading areas and other points where unauthorised persons could enter the premises should be controlled and isolated from information	Not applicable.

		processing facilities.	

Table 22: A.11.2 Equipment

ISO clause/control	Ref	Explanation	Controls
Equipment siting and protection	A.11.2.1	Equipment should be sited and protected to reduce the risks from environmental threats and hazards, and opportunities for unauthorised access.	Use Group Policies to enforce automatic time-out of user sessions if they are away from their desk for a specified period of time. Lock user workstations with a password-protected screensaver should they not use their PC for a period of time.
Supporting utilities	A.11.2.2	Equipment should be protected from power failures and other disruptions caused by failures in	Not applicable.

		supporting utilities.	
Cabling security	A.11.2.3	Power and telecommunications cabling carrying data or supporting information services should be protected from interception, interference or damage.	Ensure that all workstations are configured to use wireless networking securely. Workstations should be configured to use at least the WPA encryption protocol for connecting to wireless access points.
Equipment maintenance	A.11.2.4	Equipment should be correctly maintained to ensure its continued availability and integrity.	Use Microsoft® System Center to monitor for any potential issues that may require intervention from suppliers.
Removal of assets	A.11.2.5	Equipment, information or software should not be taken off-site without prior authorisation.	You could employ Microsoft® Systems Center 2007 to regularly scan your network to detect if any

			computers or workstations have been removed.
Security of equipment off-premises	A.11.2.6	Security should be applied to off-site assets taking into account the different risks of working outside the organisation's premises.	Ensure that all laptops, etc. utilise BitLocker™ and BitLocker To Go™ to encrypt sensitive files and data.
Secure disposal or reuse of equipment	A.11.2.7	All equipment containing storage media should be verified to ensure that any sensitive data and licenced software has been removed or securely overwritten prior to disposal or reuse.	The Microsoft® Windows® Sysinternals secure delete tool SDelete29 can be used to ensure that sensitive information is removed from any electronic devices.
Unattended user equipment	A.11.2.8	Users should ensure that unattended	Use Group Policies to enforce a

---

[29] SDelete is available from *http://technet.microsoft.com/en-us/sysinternals/bb897443.aspx*.

		equipment has appropriate protection.	password-protected screensaver after a predetermined time of inactivity. Configure the system to force users off the system should their idle time exceed a preset time limit. You can also configure the system to only allow users to log on to the network at certain times of the day. Once those times expire, the system can forcibly log the user out of the system.
Clear desk and clear screen policy	A.11.2.9	A clear desk policy for papers and removable storage media and a clear screen policy for	Configure the system to force users off the system should their idle time exceed a preset time limit.

		information processing facilities should be adopted.	The policy can be shared and displayed using Microsoft® IIS server.

Section A.12 Operations security

Table 23: A.12.1 Operational procedures and responsibilities

ISO clause/control	Ref	Explanation	Controls
Documented operating procedures	A.12.1.1	Operating procedures should be documented and made available to all users who need them.	IIS server can be used as a repository for all operational processes and procedures. Microsoft® Systems Center Manager can be used to manage the environment.
Change management	A.12.1.2	Changes to the organisation, business processes, information processing facilities and systems that affect	Microsoft® System Center can be used to manage all changes to the environment. Microsoft® Baseline Security Analyzer can

		information security should be controlled.	be used to detect if any updated software has been installed on any machines.
Capacity management	A.12.1.3	The use of resources should be monitored, tuned and projections made of future capacity requirements to ensure the required system performance.	Use Microsoft® System Center to monitor for performance- and/or capacity-related issues. Use Reliability and Performance monitor within Windows Server® 2008 to monitor and detect any performance or capacity issues. Use Microsoft® System Center Capacity Planner to create capacity planning models for Exchange Server.

			Use failover clustering to ensure capacity demands can be maintained despite adversity.
Separation of development, testing and operational environments	A.12.1.4	Development, testing and operational environments should be separated to reduce the risks of unauthorised access or changes to the operational environment.	User groups can be employed at the domain level to separate the duties of users from various teams and to restrict permissions and file access rights to prevent any unauthorised changes to systems. Enable auditing to track the activity of users on the systems.

Table 24: A.12.2 Protection from malware

ISO clause/control	Ref	Explanation	Controls
Controls against malware	A.12.2.1	Detection, prevention and recovery controls to protect against malware should be implemented, combined with appropriate user awareness.	Install Microsoft® Forefront™ Antivirus on all workstations and servers. Ensure Microsoft® Defender is running on all machines. Ensure that all systems have the latest patches by either using the Windows® Update Service or centrally managing all updates using Windows® System Update Service. Restricting user access rights to only what they require and not providing elevated privileges can prevent malicious software infecting a machine. Ensure that the

			firewall built into Windows® 7 and Windows Server® 2008 is turned on and configured correctly.
			Deploy Microsoft® Forefront™ Threat Management Gateway at the network perimeter to control access to the network.
			Install Forefront™ Security for Exchange Server to detect and prevent malicious software.
			Install the Junk filter option within Microsoft® Outlook.
			Disable Automatic Preview of emails in Microsoft® Outlook. This prevents the email being automatically opened and any code in it being executed.
			Disable Automatic

				opening of Next Message in Microsoft® Outlook. This prevents the user from inadvertently opening an email containing a malicious payload.
				Disable processing of active content within Microsoft® Outlook.
				Configure 'security zones' for Microsoft® Outlook so that:
				• Downloading signed ActiveX® controls is disabled
				• Downloading unsigned ActiveX® controls is disabled
				• Java™ permissions are disabled
				• Launching programs within an IFRAME is disabled

			<ul><li>Active scripting is disabled</li><li>Scripting of Java™ applets is disabled.</li></ul>Configure Internet Explorer® to browse the Internet securely. Download and review the Security Monitoring and Attack Detection Planning Guide.[30] Regularly scan all systems for vulnerabilities using Microsoft® Security Baseline Advisor. Deploy Microsoft® Network Access Protection to ensure only devices with the appropriate patch levels, anti-virus software and security

---

[30]

www.microsoft.com/technet/security/guidance/auditingandmonitoring/securitymonitoring /default.mspx.

			configurations can access your network. Turn on anti-spam filters on the Microsoft® Exchange Server. Alternatively, you could deploy Microsoft® Forefront™ for Exchange which has more comprehensive anti-spam and anti-virus controls. System Center

Table 25: A.12.3 Backup

ISO clause/control	Ref	Explanation	Controls
Information back-up	A.12.3.1	Backup copies of information, software and system images should be taken and tested regularly in accordance with an	You could deploy Microsoft® System Center to manage all server back-ups. You could configure the back-up features within Microsoft® Windows® 7 and Windows Server® 2008 to regularly back up critical

		agreed backup policy.	system and data files.

Table 26: A.12.4 Logging and monitoring

ISO clause/control	Ref	Explanation	Controls
Event logging	A.12.4.1	Event logs recording user activities, exceptions, faults and information security events should be produced, kept and regularly reviewed.	Ensure that audit logging is turned on. *Please refer to Chapter 8 for more details.* Dynamic Access Control allows logging of information access for audit.
Protection of log information	A.12.4.2	Logging facilities and log information should be protected against tampering and unauthorised access.	Ensure that appropriate permissions are set on the folders that store the log files to protect them. Restrict access to the log files to those authorised to view them. Servers should be configured to shut down

			should the security log become full.
Administrator and operator logs	A.12.4.3	System administrator and system operator activities should be logged and the logs protected and regularly reviewed.	Use IIS server to log all operator and admin staff activity.
Clock synchronisation	A.12.4.4	The clocks of all relevant information processing systems within the organisation or security domain should be synchronised to a single reference time source.	Configure one server on your network to be your internal time server. Ensure that server is synchronising with a reputable external network time server.31 Configure all other servers and critical network devices to source their time from your internal network

---

31 For more information, see *www.nist.gov/physlab/div847/grp40/its.cfm*.

			time server.

Table 27: A.12.5 Control of operational software

ISO clause/control	Ref	Explanation	Controls
Installation of software on operational systems	A.12.5.1	Procedures should be implemented to control the installation of software on operational systems.	Ensure only certain users have appropriate permissions to make changes to system and production files. Use Microsoft® Systems Center to manage rollout of software into production. Use built-in back-up utilities to back up the system before any changes are made. Use AppLocker™ to provide access to restrict users to the applications they need for their job role.

Table 28: A.12.6 Technical vulnerability management

ISO clause/control	Ref	Explanation	Controls
Management of technical vulnerabilities	A.12.6.1	Information about technical vulnerabilities of information systems being used should be obtained in a timely fashion, the organisation's exposure to such vulnerabilities evaluated and appropriate measures taken to address the associated risk.	Subscribe to the Microsoft Security Response Blog: *blogs.technet.com/msrc/*. Subscribe to Microsoft's Malware Protection Center: *www.microsoft.com/security/sir/default.aspx* Employ the Microsoft® Baseline Security Analyzer to regularly scan for known vulnerabilities.
Restrictions on software installation	A.12.5.4	Rules governing the installation of software by users should be established and implemented.	All sensitive information should be stored on secure shares and where necessary those shares encrypted using BitLocker™.

			Use Active Directory® Rights Management Services to manage who has access to the data and what they can do with the data.
			Use Microsoft® Systems Center 2007 to regularly monitor the network and server processes and services that could indicate malicious activity.
			Ensure only certain users have appropriate permissions to make changes to system and production files.
			Use Microsoft® Systems Center to manage rollout of software into production.
			Use AppLocker™ to

			provide access to restrict users to the applications they need for their job role.

Table 29: A.12.7 Information systems audit considerations

ISO clause/control	Ref	Explanation	Controls
Information system audit controls	A.12.7.1	Audit requirements and activities involving verification of operational systems should be carefully planned and agreed to minimise disruptions to business processes.	All audits can be scheduled and published via either IIS server or shared diaries within Microsoft® Exchange.

Section A.13 Communications security

Table 30: A.13.1 Network security management

ISO clause/control	Ref	Explanation	Controls
Network controls	A.13.1.1	Networks should be managed and	You could employ Windows®

		controlled to protect information in systems and applications.	Network Access Protection to ensure only machines that meet your security criteria can connect to the network.
			You could configure network clients and servers to use IPsec to communicate over the network.
			Employ DirectAccess for remote users to access the corporate network.
Security of network services	A.13.1.2	Security mechanisms, service levels and management requirements of all network services should be identified and included in network services	Regularly scan network devices with Microsoft® Baseline Security Advisor for any known vulnerabilities.

		agreements, whether these services are provided in-house or outsourced.	
Segregation in networks	A.13.1.3	Groups of information services, users and information systems should be segregated on networks.	You could use IPsec to segregate secure network traffic and servers from other systems. Use Microsoft® Forefront™ Threat Management Gateway to protect the perimeter of your network from unauthorised traffic. In a high-security environment you could also use Microsoft® Forefront™ Threat Management Gateway as a firewall to further segregate sensitive servers from your own internal network.

| | | | | Regularly review the user accounts database to ensure that users are in appropriate groups with the relevant permissions for their current role and that accounts for staff no longer working for the organisation have been removed. |
| | | | | Ensure firewalls built into Microsoft® Windows® 7/8 and Windows Server® 2008/2012 are turned on and configured correctly. |

Table 31: A.13.2 Information transfer

ISO clause/control	Ref	Explanation	Controls
Information transfer policies and procedures	A.13.2.1	Formal transfer policies, procedures and controls should	Regularly scan network devices with Microsoft® Baseline

		be in place to protect the transfer of information through the use of all types of communication facilities.	Security Advisor for any known vulnerabilities.
Agreements on information transfer	A.13.3.2	Agreements should address the secure transfer of business information between the organisation and external parties.	Use IIS to provide people with a central point to ensure they understand what the contents of any exchange agreements are. If your partner organisation is also using Windows Server® 2008 you could use Active Directory® Rights Management Services to manage the handling of sensitive data. Store sensitive data in secure network shares with appropriate permissions

			assigned.
Electronic messaging	A.13.2.3	Information involved in electronic messaging shall be appropriately protected.	Ensure that you set up and configure Microsoft® Exchange securely.
Confidentiality or non-disclosure agreements	A.13.2.4	Requirements for confidentiality or non-disclosure agreements reflecting the organisation's needs for the protection of information should be identified, regularly reviewed and documented.	A standard confidentiality agreement could be developed as a template in Microsoft® Office and shared using Microsoft® IIS server. Active Directory® Rights Management Services could be used to ensure only authorised copies of the document are available.

Section A.14 System acquisition, development and maintenance

Table 32: A.14.1 Security requirements of information systems

ISO clause/control	Ref	Explanation	Controls
Information security requirements analysis and specification	A.14.1.1	The information security related requirements should be included in the requirements for new information systems or enhancements to existing information systems.	Use the Microsoft® Threat Analysis and Modeling Enterprise Edition tool to identify any security risks and threats in the proposed system.
Securing application services on public networks	A.14.1.2	Information involved in application services passing over public networks should be protected from fraudulent activity,	Employ Active Directory® Certificate Services to create cryptographic keys to encrypt all data from your server to the clients. Ensure appropriate controls are on

		contract dispute and unauthorised disclosure and modification.	the server so that only authorised personnel can change any settings, data or pricing on the server. Use Microsoft® Systems Center to monitor for any unusual activity on the system.
Protecting application services transactions	A.14.1.3	Information involved in application service transactions shall be protected to prevent incomplete transmission, mis-routing, unauthorised message alteration, unauthorised disclosure, unauthorised message duplication or replay.	Employ Active Directory® Certificate Services to create cryptographic keys to encrypt all data from your server to the clients. Ensure appropriate controls are on the server so that only authorised personnel can change any settings, data or pricing. Use Microsoft® Systems Center to monitor for any unusual

			activity on the system.

Table 33: A.14.2 Security in development and support processes

ISO clause/control	Ref	Explanation	Controls
Secure development policy	A.14.2.1	Rules for the development of software and systems should be established and applied to developments within the organisation.	The following tools can be used to minimise the risk of insecure coding: You can use Microsoft® Baseline Security Analyzer to ensure no vulnerabilities are introduced into the system. The Microsoft® Source Code Analyzer for SQL Injection can be used to test the applications to ensure no vulnerabilities are introduced. Microsoft® CAT.NET code analysis tool for

			managed code tries to identify where input validation attacks can occur.
System change control procedures	A.14.2.2	Changes to systems within the development lifecycle should be controlled by the use of formal change control procedures.	A documented change control process can be published and shared on the IIS server. Microsoft® Systems Center could be employed to manage changes to the production environment.
Technical review of applications after operating platform changes	A.12.5.2	When operating platforms are changed, business critical applications should be reviewed and tested to ensure there is no adverse impact on organisational	You can use Microsoft® Baseline Security Analyzer to ensure no new vulnerabilities have been introduced into the system. The Microsoft® Source Code Analyzer for SQL Injection can be used to test the

		operations or security.	applications to ensure no new vulnerabilities were introduced.
Restrictions on changes to software packages	A.12.5.3	Modifications to software packages should be discouraged, limited to necessary changes and all changes should be strictly controlled.	Ensure that only authorised users have access to the software packages. Microsoft® System Center could be used to monitor for any changes to software. Audit trails and event logs can be reviewed regularly to identify if any unauthorised changes or access occurred. Use AppLocker™ to provide access to restrict users to the applications they need for their job role.
Secure system engineering principles	A.12.2.1	Principles for engineering secure systems should be	The following tools can be used to ensure the system is performing as it

		established, documented, maintained and applied to any information system implementatio n efforts.	should: The Microsoft® Threat Analysis and Modeling Enterprise Edition to ensure that any recommended changes have been implemented. Microsoft® CAT.NET code analysis tool for managed code that tries to identify where input validation attacks can occur. The Microsoft® Source Code Analyzer for SQL Injection is a static code analysis tool for finding SQL injection vulnerabilities in ASP code.
Secure development environment	A.14.2.6	Organisation should establish and appropriately	Ensure that only authorised users have access to the development

		protect secure development environments for system development and integration efforts that cover the entire system development lifecycle.	environment. Use Microsoft® Systems Center to manage the development environment.
Outsourced development	A.14.2.7	The organisation should supervise and monitor the activity of outsourced system development.	Use the Microsoft® Threat Analysis and Modeling Enterprise Edition to ensure that any recommended changes have been implemented. Use Microsoft® CAT.NET code analysis tool for managed code that tries to identify where input validation attacks can occur. The Microsoft® Source Code Analyzer for

			SQL Injection is a static code analysis tool for finding SQL injection vulnerabilities in ASP code.
System security testing	A.14.2.8	Testing of security functionality should be carried out during development.	Use the Microsoft® Threat Analysis and Modeling Enterprise Edition to ensure that any recommended changes have been implemented. Use Microsoft® CAT.NET code analysis tool for managed code that tries to identify where input validation attacks can occur. The Microsoft® Source Code Analyzer for SQL Injection is a static code analysis tool for finding SQL injection

			vulnerabilities in ASP code.
System acceptance testing	A.14.2.9	Acceptance testing programs and related criteria should be established for new information systems, upgrades and new versions.	Test all systems are up to date and patched before implementing into production using Microsoft® Baseline Security Analyzer. Use Microsoft® Systems Center to ensure systems meet agreed minimum requirements

Table 34: A.14.3 Test data

ISO clause/control	Ref	Explanation	Controls
Protection of test data	A.14.3.1	Test data should be selected carefully, protected and controlled.	You should isolate test data away from production systems and ensure the test data is stored on a secure share or database on a server with the appropriate permissions.

			Permissions to the test data should be set for only those authorised to view that data.

Section A.15 Supplier relationships

Table 35: A.15.1 Information security in supplier relationships

ISO clause/control	Ref	Explanation	Controls
Information security policy for supplier relationships	A.15.1.1	Information security requirements for mitigating the risks associated with supplier's access to the organisation's assets should be agreed with the supplier and documented.	Use the Microsoft® Security Assessment Tool. Regularly test remote connections with Microsoft® Baseline Security Analyzer to ensure latest vulnerabilities are installed. Ensure event logging is turned on for all servers providing remote access.
Addressing	A.6.2.3	All relevant	Use the

security within third-party agreements		information security requirements should be established and agreed with each supplier that may access, process, store, communicate, or provide IT infrastructure components for, the organisation's information.	Microsoft® Security Assessment Tool. Regularly test remote connections with Microsoft® Baseline Security Analyzer to ensure latest vulnerabilities are installed. Ensure event logging is turned on for all servers providing remote access.
Information and communication technology supply chain	A.15.1.3	Agreements with suppliers should include requirements to address the information security risks associated with information and communications technology services and	Use the Microsoft® Security Assessment Tool. Regularly test remote connections with Microsoft® Baseline Security Analyzer to ensure latest vulnerabilities are installed.

		product supply chain.	Ensure event logging is turned on for all servers providing remote access.

Table 36: A.15.2 Supplier service delivery management

ISO clause/control	Ref	Explanation	Controls
Monitoring and review of supplier services	A.15.2.1	Organisations should regularly monitor, review and audit supplier service delivery.	Use the Microsoft® Security Assessment Tool. Regularly test remote connections with Microsoft® Baseline Security Analyzer to ensure latest vulnerabilities are installed. Ensure event logging is turned on for all servers providing remote access.
Managing changes to supplier services	A.15.2.2	Changes to the provision of services by suppliers, including	You could use Microsoft® System Center to monitor and detect any changes to the

		maintaining and improving existing information security policies, procedures and controls, should be managed, taking account of the criticality of business information, systems and processes involved and re-assessment of risks.	systems being used to manage third-party access. In addition, any required changes could be deployed using Microsoft® System Center.

Section A.16 Information security incident management

Table 37: A.16.1 Management of information security incidents and improvements

ISO clause/control	Ref	Explanation	Controls
Responsibilities and procedures	A.16.1.1	Management responsibilities and procedures should be established to	You could publish all contact details for key staff on IIS so that they

		ensure a quick, effective and orderly response to information security incidents.	are available when required.
			You could also create an email distribution group to alert the appropriate personnel.
			All processes and procedures could be shared via secured pages within IIS or on secure network shares so you can ensure only authorised personnel have access to the material.
			Use the Microsoft® Malware Removal Starter Kit.[32]
			Use the Microsoft® Antivirus

[32] www.microsoft.com/downloads/details.aspx?familyid=6cd853ce-f349-4a18-a14f-c99b64adfbea&displaylang=en.

			Defense-in-Depth Guide.[33] Use the Security Monitoring and Attack Detection Planning Guide.[34] Use the Microsoft® RootkitRevealer tool to identify rootkits on your system.[35]
Reporting information security events	A.16.1.2	Information security events should be reported through appropriate management channels as quickly as possible.	Use IIS to enable users to report security events. Create a dedicated mailbox in Microsoft® Exchange to report security events.
Reporting security weaknesses	A.16.1.3	Employees and contractors using the organisation's	Use IIS to enable users to report security events. Create a dedicated

---

[33] *www.microsoft.com/technet/security/guidance/serversecurity/avdind_0.mspx*.
[34]
www.microsoft.com/technet/security/guidance/auditingandmonitoring/securitymonitoring/default.mspx.
[35] *http://technet.microsoft.com/en-ie/sysinternals/bb897445(en-us).aspx*.

		information systems should be required to note and report any observed or suspected information security weaknesses in systems or services	mailbox in Microsoft® Exchange to report security events.
			Use reports from the following tools to highlight identified security issues:
			• Microsoft® Baseline Security Analyzer
			• Microsoft® Security Assessment Tool
			• The Microsoft® Threat Analysis and Modeling Enterprise Edition
			• Microsoft® CAT.NET code analysis tool
			• The Microsoft® Source Code

			Analyzer for SQL Injection
Assessment of and decision on information security events	A.16.1.4	Information security events should be assessed and it should be decided if they are to be classified as information security incidents.	Use the Microsoft® Security Assessment Tool. All processes and procedures could be shared via secured pages within IIS or on secure network shares so you can ensure only authorised personnel have access to the material.
Response to information security incidents	A.16.1.5	Information security incidents should be responded to in accordance with the documented procedures.	You could publish all contact details for key staff on IIS so that they are available when required. You could also create an email distribution group to alert the appropriate personnel. All processes and procedures

				could be shared via secured pages within IIS or on secure network shares so you can ensure only authorised personnel have access to the material.
				Use the Microsoft® Malicious Software Removal Tool.[36]
				Use the Microsoft® Antivirus Defense-in-Depth Guide.[37]
				Use the Security Monitoring and Attack Detection Planning Guide.[38]
				Use the Microsoft® RootkitRevealer tool to identify

---

[36] *www.microsoft.com/en-us/download/malicious-software-removal-tool-details.aspx*
[37] *http://technet.microsoft.com/library/cc162791*
[38] *http://technet.microsoft.com/library/cc163158*

			rootkits on your system.[39]
Learning from information security incidents	A.16.1.6	Knowledge gained from analysing and resolving information security incidents should be used to reduce the likelihood or impact of future incidents.	You can publish all updated procedures and policies using IIS. The Microsoft® Baseline Security Analyzer can be used to scan recovered systems to ensure that any vulnerabilities that facilitated the attack are no longer present.
Collection of evidence	A.16.1.7	The organisation should define and apply procedures for the identification, collection, acquisition and preservation of information,	Review the Microsoft Fundamental Computer Investigation Guide for Windows®.[40] You can copy all relevant Microsoft system, application and security logs to a

[39] http://technet.microsoft.com/en-us/sysinternals/bb897445.aspx
[40] http://technet.microsoft.com/en-ie/library/cc162846(en-us).aspx

			which can serve as evidence.	write-once read-many CD for preservation. For additional security, you can use Microsoft®'s File Checksum Integrity Verifier tool to create MD5 cryptographic hash signatures for marking collected evidence.[41]
				You can use the Microsoft® Baseline Security Analyzer to determine what vulnerabilities exist in a system.
				Log Parser is a free tool from Microsoft that enables you to query and access text-based data, such as that held in event logs, log files, Active Directory and

---

[41] *www.microsoft.com/en-us/download/details.aspx?id=11533*

			others.
			The following commands and utilities built into Windows® can be used to gather evidence:
			Arp: Display address resolution protocol (ARP) tables.
			Date: Display current date setting.
			Dir: Display a list of files and subdirectories.
			Doskey: Display command history for an open CMD.EXE shell.
			Ipconfig: Display local computer configuration.
			Net: Update, fix, or view the network or network settings.
			Netstat: Display protocol statistics and current connection

			information.
			Time: Display current time setting.
			Find: Search file(s) to find a string.
			Schtasks: Display scheduled tasks.
			Systeminfo: Provide general information about the computer.
			Vol: Display the disk volume label and serial number, if they exist.
			Hostname: Display the host name portion of the full computer name of the computer.
			Openfiles: Query, display or disconnect open files or files opened by network users.
			FCIV: File checksum integrity verifier.

				Use to compute an MD5 or SHA1 cryptographic hash of the content of a file.
				Notepad: Use to examine metadata associated with a file.
				Reg: Use to view, modify, export, save or delete registry keys, values and hives.
				Netcap: Gather network trace information from the command line.
				Sc: Use to communicate with the Service Controller and services. (Sc query is useful for dumping all services and their states.)
				Assoc: View or modify file name extension associations.

			Ftype: View or modify file types used in file name extension associations.
			Gpresult: Determine resulting set of policies.
			Tasklist: List running processes and loaded modules.
			Rsop.msc: Show resulting set of policies.
			Rasdiag: Collect diagnostic information about remote services and place that information in a file.
			The Microsoft® Windows® Sysinternals Tools42 have a range of utilities to support your investigation. Below are the

---

[42] http://technet.microsoft.com/en-us/sysinternals/default.aspx

			tools most relevant to incident response:
			AccessChk v5.2: Display access to files, registry keys or Windows® services by the user or group you specify.
			AccessEnum v1.32: Display who has access to which directories, files and registry keys on a computer. Use it to find places where permissions are not properly applied.
			Autoruns v11.70: Display programs that are configured to start up automatically when a computer boots and a user logs in (also displays the full list of registry

			and file locations where applications can configure auto-start settings).
			Diskmon v2.01: Capture all hard-disk activity. Acts like a software disk activity light in your system tray.
			DiskView v2.4: Graphical disk-sector utility, disk viewer.
			Du v1.5: Display disk usage by directory.
			Handle v3.51: Display open files and the process that opened those files.
			ListDLLs v3.1: Display all the DLLs that are currently loaded, including where they are loaded and their version numbers (prints the full path

				names of loaded modules).
				LogonSessions v1.21: List active logon sessions.
				PendMoves v1.2: Display file rename and delete commands that will be executed the next time the computer is started.
				Portmon v3.03: Display serial and parallel port activity (will also show a portion of the data being sent and received).
				Process Explorer v16.02: Display files, registry keys and other objects that processes have open, which DLLs they have loaded, owners of processes, etc.
				PsExec v2.11: Execute

			processes remotely.
			PsFile v1.02: Display open files.
			PsInfo v1.77: Display information about a computer.
			PsList v1.3: Display information about processes and threads.
			PsLoggedOn v1.34: Display users logged on to a computer.
			PsLogList v2.71: Dump event log records.
			PsService v2.24: View and control services.
			ShareEnum v1.6: Scan file shares on a network and view their security settings to eliminate improperly applied settings.

			Streams v1.56: Reveal NTFS alternate data streams.
			Strings v2.52: Search for ANSI and UNICODE strings in binary images.
			TCPView v3.05: Display all open TCP and UDP endpoints and the name of the process that owns each endpoint.

Section A.17 Information security aspects of business continuity management

Table 38: A.17.1 Information security continuity

ISO clause/control	Ref	Explanation	Controls
Planning information security continuity	A.17.1.1	The organisation should determine its requirements for information security and the continuity of information security management in adverse situations.	The Microsoft® Operations Framework 4.0 provides a framework for delivering IT services, including business continuity.[43] Use the Microsoft Security Risk Management Guide and the Microsoft® Security Assessment Tool to identify any risks relating to business continuity, especially the Reliability Overview section.

---

[43] *http://technet.microsoft.com/en-ie/library/cc506049(en-us).aspx*

| Implementing information security continuity | A.17.1.2 | The organisation should establish, document, implement and maintain processes, procedures and controls to ensure the required level of continuity for information security during an adverse situation. | All documented plans can be published and shared using either IIS server or network shares on the network. Implement failover clustering to ensure services and applications remain accessible during information security continuity events. |
| Verify, review and evaluate information security continuity | A.17.1.3 | The organisation should verify the established and implemented information security continuity controls at regular intervals in order to ensure that they are valid and | You can maintain your business continuity testing plan as a shared and published resource on IIS. |

| | | effective during adverse situations. | |
| | | | |

Table 39: A.17.2 Redundancies

ISO clause/control	Ref	Explanation	Controls
Availability of information processing facilities	A.17.2.1	Information processing facilities should be implemented with redundancy sufficient to meet availability requirements.	Use Microsoft® System Center to monitor for performance- and/or capacity-related issues. Use Reliability and Performance monitor within Windows Server® 2008/2012 to monitor and detect any performance or capacity issues. Use Microsoft® System Center Capacity Planner to create capacity planning models for Exchange Server. Implement failover clustering to ensure services

			and applications remain accessible during information security continuity events.

Section A.18 Compliance

Table 40: A.18.1 Compliance with legal and contractual requirements

ISO clause/control	Ref	Explanation	Controls
Identification of applicable legislation and contractual requirements	A.18.1.1	All relevant legislative, statutory, regulatory, contractual requirements and the organisation's approach to meet these requirements should be explicitly identified, documented and kept up to date for each information	A dedicated page on IIS could be used to link to the relevant legislation applicable to your organisation's business needs. In addition, the key compliance requirements for customer contracts could also be published via IIS to ensure all relevant users are aware of the key points. You could also store soft copies of the

		system and the organisation	contracts in a secure network share for authorised users to review.
Intellectual property rights	A.18.1.2	Appropriate procedures should be implemented to ensure compliance with legislative, regulatory and contractual requirements related to intellectual property rights and use of proprietary software products.	You can use Microsoft® Systems Center to regularly scan the network to ensure only authorised copies of software are installed. Use AppLocker™ to provide access to restrict users to the applications they need for their job role.
Protection of records	A.18.1.3	Records should be protected from loss, destruction, falsification, unauthorised access and unauthorised release, in	You should ensure that all electronic records are stored in secure shares with the appropriate permissions and access rights applied.

| | | accordance with legislator, regulatory, contractual and business requirements. | Regular reviews of user rights should help you identify if users have inappropriate rights to various systems. You can use Microsoft® Baseline Security Analyzer to ensure no known vulnerabilities exist on devices hosting electronic records. You should employ appropriate malware protection tools as outlined in A.10.4 Protection Against Malicious and Mobile Code. |
| Privacy and protection of personally identifiable information | A.18.1.4 | Privacy and protection of personally identifiable information | You should ensure that all electronic records are stored in secure shares with the |

		should be ensured as required in relevant legislation and regulation where applicable.	appropriate permissions and access rights applied. Regular reviews of user rights should help you identify if users have inappropriate rights to various systems. You can use Microsoft® Baseline Security Analyzer to ensure no known vulnerabilities exist on devices hosting electronic records. You should employ appropriate malware protection tools as outlined in A.12.2 Protection from, malware.
Regulation of cryptographic controls	A.18.1.5	Cryptographic controls should be used in	You should consider monitoring log files using

		compliance with all relevant agreements, legislation and regulations.	Microsoft® System Center to detect if users are using encryption tools to mask their email or Internet activity.

Table 41: A.18.2 Information security reviews

ISO clause/control	Ref	Explanation	Controls
Independent review of information security	A.18.2.1	The organisation's approach to managing information security and its implementation should be reviewed independently at planned intervals or when significant changes occur.	Use the Microsoft Security Risk Management Guide. Use the Microsoft® Security Assessment Tool.
Compliance with security policies and standards	A.18.2.2	Managers should regularly review the compliance of information	You should consider monitoring log files using Microsoft® System Center to

		processing and procedures within their area of responsibility with the appropriate security policies, standards and any other security requirements.	detect if there is any user or system activity that does not comply with the policies of your ISMS.
Technical compliance checking	A.18.2.3	Information systems should be regularly reviewed for compliance with the organisation's security policies and standards.	You should regularly check Microsoft's website for any updates to their security guides, in particular the Microsoft Security TechCenter44 and the Security and Update section on the Microsoft Technet site.45System Center.

---

[44] *http://technet.microsoft.com/en-ie/security/default(en-us).aspx*.

[45] *http://technet.microsoft.com/en-ie/library/cc498723(en-us).aspx*.

CHAPTER 8: SECURING THE WINDOWS® ENVIRONMENT

This chapter describes how best to implement the security controls that you have selected as part of your ISO27001-based ISMS.

The details in this chapter will focus on the key operating systems of Windows Server® 2008 and 2012, Windows® 7 and Windows® 8. While other Microsoft systems and applications may be referred to, the scope of this book does not provide the same level of technical detail for these other systems. Where possible, references to Microsoft resources will be made to enable the reader to research the information further.

Furthermore, the reader is advised to ensure that all recommendations outlined in this book are fully tested and compatible with their own production environment before they are set to 'live'.

Windows Server® 2008 and 2012 architecture

The following section outlines how best to secure the Windows Server® 2008 and 2012 architecture which ensures an environment that is secure yet easy to support and manage.

Structured naming convention

In order to quickly identify Windows Server® 2008 and 2012 servers and their roles within your organisation, all servers should comply with a structured naming convention. Having a structured naming convention provides a number of benefits:

- Devices are located near each other within the 'My Network' application.
- Device names within system and application logs make it easier to troubleshoot issues.
- Device names within security logs make it easier to respond to and manage security incidents.

Domain name

You should choose a domain name that is suitable for your organisation. Most organisations try and implement a single domain to provide for ease of support and management. If possible you should follow this approach.

Windows® server naming conventions

Windows® servers will adhere to the following naming convention:

Server Name = <DOMAIN>SRV<R>nn

Table 46 describes the parameters.

Table 42: Server naming parameters

Parameter	Description
<DOMAIN>	This is the domain you choose.
SRV	This indicates that this machine is a server.
<R>	This is the role of the server within the domain, for example:

	DC for domain controller
	MBR for member server
	DB for database server
	PRN for print server
	FS for file-sharing server
	DNS for DNS server
	DHCP for DHCP server
	NM for network management server
	BCK for back-up server
	WWW for Web server
	EXG for Exchange server
	FAX for network fax server
	OWA for Outlook Web access server
	APP for application server
<nn>	This is a numeric sequence number.

The above naming convention will enable ready identification of a server and its role within the network. All servers will also be listed together under the Browser service, enabling easier management and identification of a server.

Client workstation names

In order to readily identify all workstations on the network and their location, all workstations installed on your domain should adhere to a structured naming convention, such as the following:

Workstation Name = <DOMAIN><LOC><TYP><nn>

Table 47 describes the parameters.

Table 43: Workstation naming parameters

Parameter	Setting
<DOMAIN>	This is the domain name.
<LOC>	This indicates where the workstation is located, for example: ACC for the accounts dept HR for the HR dept IT for the IT dept or you could use site location: LON for London NYC for New York PAR for Paris
<TYP>	This is the type of workstation, for example: PC for a desktop PC NB for a notebook/laptop computer TC for a thin client device
<nn>	This is a numeric sequence number.

Printer names

In order for users to easily identify and recognise the printers they are printing to, to ease the technical support of the printing environment and to better secure the printers, you should also consider implementing a structured naming convention for printers, such as:

Printer Name – <LOC><TYP><MF><nn>

Table 48 describes the parameters.

Table 44: Printer naming parameters

Parameter	Setting
<LOC>	This indicates where the printer is located, for example: ACC for the accounts dept HR for the HR dept IT for the IT dept or you could use site location: LON for London NYC for New York PAR for Paris
<TYP>	This is the type of printer, for example: MLSR for a monochrome laser printer CLSR for a colour laser printer INK for an ink-jet printer
<MF>	This is the manufacturer of the printer: IBM for IBM HP for Hewlett Packard DELL for Dell LEX for Lexmark XER for Xerox
<nn>	This is a numeric sequence number.

Domain user accounts naming standards

User accounts

All user accounts in use within your organisation should be domain accounts and not local accounts held on the Windows® workstation's local user account database. Having all user accounts as domain accounts will enable administrators of the domain to better manage, support and secure the user accounts.

The standard naming convention for user accounts should be designed on a structured basis to facilitate ease of management and support. A common structure used by a lot of organisations is based on the following:

Account Name = <LastName><FirstNameInitial>

This means that the user account will be composed of the user's surname and the initial for their forename, e.g. John Smith would have a username of SmithJ. If there is a conflict in the name generated, however, the first character of the user's middle name could be appended. For example:

John Smith = SmithJM

Jane Smith = SmithJ

There are many other user account naming conventions; it is important that whatever basis you choose should be capable of handling growth and change in the number of users, as well as overlap between user names.

Windows Server® 2008 and 2012 domain administrator account

As all Windows Server® 2008 and 2012 installations have an account called Administrator by default. Because this is the most interesting account for anyone trying to attack the server, it is recommended that you rename the built-in Administrator account to something that is not as easily identifiable, i.e. it should not be called Admin or Supervisor.

As the administrator is the one account that can never be locked out due to repeated failed logon attempts, changing the account name will force malicious users attempting to log on with this account to guess not only the correct password (which should be an impressively strong password) but also the correct account name.

For additional security, it is best to copy the logon details of this account twice and hold them in two physically separate secure places. This account should only be used in an emergency. Only a limited number of authorised personnel should have access to the administrator account.

For the daily administration of the domain, you should create named user accounts with the same permissions as the administrator account. These accounts can then be used by those responsible for administrating the Windows® server domain. Requiring these individuals to use unique accounts to administer the domain also makes it easy for you to ensure segregation of duties and also to track in the logs and audit trails which person made any particular changes to the system. If everyone is using the one shared administrator account, you would not have the same level of control.

In line with the earlier recommended user account naming standard, you should consider a similar naming convention for these domain administrator accounts based on the following:

Account Name = ADMIN<LastName><FirstNameInitial>

This means that the account will be composed from the user's surname and the initial for their forename, e.g. John Smith would have a username of SmithJ. The prefix ADMIN will indicate that this account is an administrative account. If there is a conflict in the name generated, the first character of the user's middle name could be appended. For example, the account names for the domain administrators John Michael Smith and Jane Smith are:

John Smith = ADMINSmithJM

Jane Smith = ADMINSmithJ

The renamed administrator account will be available in the event of an equivalent administrator account(s) becoming corrupt or the password for that account(s) being forgotten.

Service-desk administration

Many organisations allow their service-desk personnel to have administrative access to the domain in order to manage and support the end-users and their computers. With the flexibility of user rights within Windows Server® 2008 and 2012, however, you can lock down the level of access your service-desk personnel have to your network. Any members of your service desk who will be tasked with administrating the domain can have their accounts made members of a special group that can be named 'Service Desk Administrators'. To enable your service-desk personnel to perform their duties, you can make the Security Desk Administrators group members of the following Windows® domain groups:

- Account operators
- Server operators
- Backup operators
- Print operators.

By adding the service-desk administrator accounts into the above groups, you will allow your service-desk personnel to conduct their daily administrative tasks, such as managing user accounts and managing shares on servers.

Guest account

Under no circumstances should you allow the Guest account to be enabled. Clients who are not members of your organisation and who require access to resources on your domain should be given a valid, temporary user account.

In addition to disabling the Guest account, you should also rename it to an account whose details are not easy to guess.

Everyone group

By default the Everyone group is given access to any new directories and shares that are set up under Windows Server®. Therefore, inappropriate or incorrect use of the Everyone group could be potentially exploited to allow non-authorised clients to access resources on your network.

For example, if the Guest account is enabled, and because the Guest account is part of the Everyone group, the Guest account will have access to anything that the Everyone group has access to. When setting up a new share, access to the share should be removed from the Everyone group. A more preferable group to use for a new share is the Domain Users group.

CHAPTER 9: SECURING THE MICROSOFT® WINDOWS SERVER® PLATFORM

Critical to the overall security of your network will be ensuring the security of the Windows Server® 2008 or 2012 platform that provides a range of services to your client base.

There are two types of server that will need to be considered when looking at securing the Windows Server® 2008 or 2012 platform. These are:

- Domain controllers
- Member servers.

Domain controllers

A network based on Windows Server® 2008 or 2012 technology stores all of its information about users, computers and other devices on the network in what is called Active Directory® Services. In order to manage the details stored within the Active Directory® devices, Windows Server® 2008 and 2012 use domain controllers. Domain controllers form the core of the Windows® network and are essential to its availability and security. When a user logs on to the network, their logon is processed by a domain controller which will check and verify that the user's credentials are valid and what access they should have to the domain.

Read-only domain controller

A feature of Windows Server® 2008 and 2012 is the read-only domain controller (RODC). In earlier versions of Windows Server®, you had two choices with regard to authenticating users in remote offices. The first was to enable remote clients to authenticate their log-ins over the wide area network but this would often prove to be unusable due to bandwidth issues. The second was to install a domain controller locally into the remote office to cater for the log-in requirements of the local users. The concern with this scenario is that the physical security of the domain controller in the remote office may not be as stringent as that in the head office. Anybody with physical access to the remote domain controller could simply take the server off-line and make changes to the Active Directory®, such as adding in a new account with domain administrator privileges. Once the remote domain controller was brought back online, the new administrator account would be replicated from the remote domain controller to all domain controllers in the domain, giving the unauthorised person full access to the domain.

With Windows Server® 2008 and 2012 you can now deploy a read-only domain controller. While this read-only domain controller will have changes made to user accounts and computers propagated to it via Active Directory® replication, it cannot have its local copy of Active Directory® edited or changed in any way. This offers a more secure solution for providing domain access to users in remote offices.

Member servers

For the purposes of this book we will discuss how to configure the security features of Windows Server® 2008 and 2012 in two scenarios.

Standard servers

Standard servers will provide a range of services to your network but, based on your risk assessment, may not require any major security requirements. These servers do not require any specific security settings and may run services or host information that are considered to be not high risk in line with your risk assessment.

Sensitive servers

Sensitive servers will provide services or host resources that you have identified through your risk assessment will contain sensitive or confidential information assets and therefore will require additional security above and beyond that required for standard servers. Typically, servers that would fall into this category would be those running:

- Microsoft® Internet Information Services
- Microsoft® SQL Server®
- Microsoft® Forefront™ Threat Management Gateway
- Microsoft® Exchange Server
- Servers hosting sensitive or confidential information.

Note, however, that the more restrictive the settings, the higher the risk of applications or services not interoperating properly. Before you apply any changes, you should ensure that adequate research and testing has been undertaken on the impact the proposed changes will have on the functionality of the server you are about to change. Keep in mind also that other servers and services may depend on the element that you are proposing to change, so it is important that you ensure your changes do not adversely impact on them.

Recommended settings[46]

The following recommended settings are to help you secure your Microsoft® Windows Server® 2008 or 2012 platform. The recommendations below are based on the guides provided by Microsoft, The Center for Internet Security, The SANS Institute and the US National Institute of Standards and Technology. Please refer to Appendix 2 for more details on these resources.

Table 45: Service pack and patch levels

Parameter	Setting
Current Service Pack installed (Windows Server® 2008)	Yes – Current Service Pack available[47] is Service Pack 2
Latest update rollup (Windows Server® 2012)	Yes – Latest update rollup available[48] is April 2013
Patches recognised by the Microsoft® Baseline Security Analyzer Utility	Yes

---

[46] Appendix 1 contains descriptions and explanation for each of the settings provided in the tables.
[47] As of May 2014, when this edition was written.
[48] As of May 2014, when this edition was written.

Table 46: User account policy

Parameter	Setting
Minimum password length for sensitive accounts	12 characters
Minimum password length for standard user accounts	8 characters
Maximum password age	90 days
Minimum password age	1 day
Prompt user to change password before expiration	14 days
Password complexity	Enabled
Password history	24 passwords remembered
Store passwords using reversible encryption	Disabled

Table 47: Account lockout policy

Parameter	Settings
Account lockout	Yes
Lockout after	5 failed attempts
Reset count after	30 minutes
Lockout duration	Forever (until Administrator unlocks)
Forcibly disconnect remote user from server when logon hours expire	Yes
Users must log on in order to change password	No

CHAPTER 10: AUDITING AND MONITORING

Microsoft® Windows Server® 2008 and 2012 provide a comprehensive range of auditing and logging features. If configured correctly, these features will enable you to trace all user activity on your systems in the event you need to investigate technical or security incidents.

The following sections outline some recommendations on how best to audit your Windows Server® 2008 or 2012 environment.

The recommendations below are based on the guides provided by Microsoft, The Center for Internet Security, The SANS Institute and the US National Institute of Standards and Technology. Please refer to Appendix 2 for more details on these resources.

Table 48: Configuring registry auditing

Parameter	Settings
%SystemDrive%	Failures
HKLM\Software	Failures
HKLM\System	Failures

Table 49: Configuring system auditing

Parameter	Settings
Security system extension	Success and Failure
System integrity	Success and Failure
IPsec driver	Success and Failure
Other system events	Success and Failure
Security state change	Success and Failure

Table 50: Configuring logon/logoff auditing

Parameter	Settings
Logon	Success and Failure
Logoff	Success
Account lockout	Success
IPsec main mode	No auditing
IPsec quick mode	No auditing
IPsec extended mode	No auditing
Special logon	Success
Other logon/logoff events	No auditing
Network policy server	No auditing

Table 51: Configuring auditing for objects

Parameters	Setting
File system	Failure
Registry	Failure
Kernel object	No auditing
SAM	No auditing
Certification services	No auditing
Application generated	No auditing
Handle manipulation	No auditing
File share	No auditing
Filtering platform packet drop	No auditing
Filtering platform connection	No auditing
Other object access events	No auditing

Table 52: Configuring auditing of privileges use

Parameters	Settings
Sensitive privilege use	Success and Failure
Non-sensitive privilege use	No auditing
Other Privilege Use Events	No auditing

Table 53: Configuring auditing for detailed tracking

Parameters	Settings
Process termination	No auditing
DPAPI activity	No auditing
RPC events	No auditing
Process creation	Success

Table 54: Configuring auditing for auditing policy change

Parameters	Settings
Audit policy change	Success and Failure
Authentication policy change	Success
Authorization policy change	No auditing
MPSSVC rule-level policy change	No auditing
Filtering platform policy change	No auditing
Other policy change events	No auditing

Table 55: Configuring auditing for account management

Parameters	Settings
User account management	Success and Failure
Computer account management	Success and Failure
Security group management	Success and Failure
Distribution group management	No auditing
Application group management	No auditing
Other account management events	Success and Failure

Table 56: Configuring auditing for directory service

Parameters	Settings
Directory service access	Success and Failure
Directory service changes	Success and Failure
Directory service replication	No auditing
Detailed directory service replication	No auditing

Table 57: Configuring auditing for account logon

Parameters	Settings
Kerberos authentication service	No auditing
Credential validation	Success and Failure
Kerberos service ticket operations	No auditing
Other account logon events	No auditing

Note the parameters above that are set for 'no auditing' can be turned on in the event that you are troubleshooting or conducting investigations into suspicious activity. Be aware, however, that these parameters will significantly increase the amount of logging overhead on the monitored systems. Therefore they must be deployed with care as they can have a negative impact on the performance of your servers.

Configuring auditing of file and resource access

Table 58 outlines recommended settings for access to shared folders on the server's file system. You should alter these policies depending on the needs of your organisation.

Table 58: Settings for shared folders

File/Directory audit policy	Success	Failure
Read		X
Write		X
Execute		X
Delete	X	X
Change permissions	X	X
Take ownership	X	X

Event log settings

Within Microsoft® Windows Server® 2008 and 2012 there are three main event logs that the operating system uses to record significant events:

- Application log
- System log
- Security log.

Tables 59 to 61 show the recommended settings for each of the above event logs.

Table 59: Application log settings

Parameter	Settings
Maximum event log size	16 MB
Restrict Guest access	Enabled
Log retention method	Do not overwrite (clear logs manually)
Log retention	Not applicable

Table 60: Security log settings

Parameter	Settings
Maximum event log size	80 MB
Restrict Guest access	Enabled
Log retention method	Do not overwrite (clear logs manually)
Log retention	Not applicable

Table 61: System log settings

Parameter	Settings
Maximum event log size	16 MB
Restrict Guest access	Enabled
Log retention method	Do not overwrite (clear logs manually)
Log retention	Not applicable

Events to record

The following are some of the key events that you should consider monitoring for within your event logs.

Local logon attempt failures

- Event ID 529 – Unknown user name or bad password.
- Event ID 530 – Account logon time restriction violation.
- Event ID 531 – Account currently disabled.
- Event ID 532 – The specified user account has expired.
- Event ID 533 – User not allowed to logon at this computer.
- Event ID 534 – The user has not been granted the requested logon type at this machine.
- Event ID 537 – An unexpected error occurred during logon.

Domain logon account failures

- Event ID 675 – Pre-authentication failed.
- Event ID 677 – Service ticket request failed.

Account misuse

- Event ID 530 – Account logon time restriction violation.
- Event ID 531 – Account currently disabled.
- Event ID 532 – The specified user account has expired.
- Event ID 533 – User not allowed to logon at this computer.

Account lockout

- Event ID 539 – Account locked out.

Terminal services

- Event ID 682 – Session reconnected to winstation.
- Event ID 683 – Session disconnected from winstation.

Creation of a user account

- Event ID 624 – User account created.
- Event ID 626 – User account enabled.

User account password change

- Event ID 627 – Change password attempt.
- Event ID 628 – User account password set.

User account status change

- Event ID 626 – User account enabled.
- Event ID 629 – User account disabled.
- Event ID 630 – User account deleted.

Modification of security groups

- Event ID 632 – Global group member added.
- Event ID 633 – Global group member removed.
- Event ID 636 – Local group member added.
- Event ID 637 – Local group member removed.

Modification of security log

- Event ID 517 - The audit log was cleared.

Policy change

- Event ID 608 – User right assigned.
- Event ID 609 – User right removed.
- Event ID 612 – Audit policy change.

Process tracking

Note due to the volume of log entries created when using process tracking, it is recommended to only use this feature during an investigation.

- Event ID 592 – A new process has been created.
- Event ID 593 – A process has exited.

CHAPTER 11: SECURING YOUR SERVERS

The following chapter outlines how you can enhance the security of your servers running Microsoft® Windows Server® 2008 or 2012.

To make these changes will require administrator access to the target systems. Note that some of the suggested settings may impact on certain applications or network services, particularly those provided by parties other than Microsoft. Therefore you should test each change thoroughly on a test system before introducing it into your production environment.

The recommendations below are based on the guides provided by Microsoft, The Center for Internet Security, The SANS Institute and the US National Institute of Standards and Technology. Please refer to *Appendix 2* for more details on these resources.

Table 62: Recommended security settings

Parameter	Secure server settings	Normal server settings	Registry setting
Administrator account status	Disabled	Disabled	N/A
Guest account status	Disabled	Disabled	N/A
Limit local account use of blank passwords to console only	Enabled	Enabled	MACHINE \System\Cu rrentContro lSet\Contro l\Lsa\Limit BlankPass wordUse
Rename Administrator account	Rename as discussed in Chapter 8	Rename as discussed in Chapter 8	N/A
Rename Guest account	Rename as discussed in Chapter 8	Rename as discussed in Chapter 8	N/A
Audit the access of global system objects	Default	Default	MACHINE \System\Cu rrentContro lSet\Contro l\Lsa\Audit BaseObject s
Audit the use of Backup and Restore	Enabled	Enabled	MACHINE \System\Cu rrentContro

Parameter	Secure server settings	Normal server settings	Registry setting
privileges			lSet\Control\Lsa\FullPrivilegeAuditing
Force audit policy subcategory settings (Windows® 7 or later) to override audit policy category settings	Enabled	Enabled	MACHINE\System\CurrentControlSet\Control\Lsa\SCENoApplyLegacyAuditPolicy
Shut down system immediately if unable to log security events	Enabled	Default	MACHINE\System\CurrentControlSet\Control\Lsa\CrashOnAuditFail
Allow undock without having to log on	Disabled	Disabled	MACHINE\Software\Microsoft\Windows\CurrentVersion\Policies\

Parameter	Secure server settings	Normal server settings	Registry setting
			System\Un dockWitho utLogon
Allowed to format and eject removable media	Administrators	Administrators	MACHINE \Software\ Microsoft\ Windows NT\Current Version\ Winlogon\ AllocateD ASD
Prevent users from installing print drivers	Enabled	Enabled	MACHINE \System\Cu rrentContro lSet\Contro l\Print\Prov iders\LanM an Print Services\Se rvers\AddP rinterDrive rs
Restrict CD-ROM access to locally logged-on users only	Enabled	Default	MACHINE \Software\ Microsoft\ Windows NT\Current

Parameter	Secure server settings	Normal server settings	Registry setting
			Version\ Winlogon\ AllocateC DRoms
Restrict floppy disk access to locally logged-on users only	Enabled	Default	MACHINE \Software\ Microsoft\ Windows NT\Current Version\ Winlogon\ AllocateFl oppies
Allow Server Operators to schedule tasks	Disabled	Default	
LDAP server signing requirements	Require signing	Default	
Refuse Machine account password changes	Disabled	Default	
Digitally encrypt or sign secure channel data (always)	Enabled	Enabled	MACHINE \System\Cu rrentContro lSet\Servic

Parameter	Secure server settings	Normal server settings	Registry setting
			es\Netlogo n\Paramete rs\ RequireSig nOrSeal
Digitally encrypt secure channel data	Enabled	Enabled	MACHINE \System\Cu rrentContro lSet\Servic es\Netlogo n\Paramete rs\SealSecu reChannel
Digitally sign secure channel data	Enabled	Enabled	MACHINE \System\Cu rrentContro lSet\Servic es\Netlogo n\Paramete rs\SignSec ureChannel
Disable Machine account password changes	Disabled	Disabled	MACHINE \System\Cu rrentContro lSet\Servic es\Netlogo n\Paramete rs\

Parameter	Secure server settings	Normal server settings	Registry setting
			DisablePas swordChan ge
Maximum Machine account password age	30 days	30 days	MACHINE \System\Cu rrentContro lSet\Servic es\Netlogo n\Paramete rs\ Maximum PasswordA ge
Require strong (Windows® 2000 or later) session key	Enabled	Enabled	MACHINE \System\Cu rrentContro lSet\Servic es\Netlogo n\Paramete rs\ RequireStr ongKey
Do not display last user name for interactive logon	Enabled	Enabled	MACHINE \Software\ Microsoft\ Windows\ CurrentVer sion\Polici

Parameter	Secure server settings	Normal server settings	Registry setting
			es\ System\Do ntDisplayL astUserNa me
Do not require Ctrl+Alt+Del	Disabled	Disabled	MACHINE \Software\ Microsoft\ Windows\ CurrentVer sion\Polici es\ System\Dis ableCAD
Message text for users attempting to logon	You should define the message that you wish your users to see as they log on to the network	You should define the message that you wish your users to see as they log on to the network	MACHINE \Software\ Microsoft\ Windows\ CurrentVer sion\Polici es\ System\Le galNoticeT ext
Message title for users attempting to logon	You should define the message title that you wish	You should define the message title that you wish	MACHINE \Software\ Microsoft\ Windows\

Parameter	Secure server settings	Normal server settings	Registry setting
	your users to see as they log on to the network	your users to see as they log on to the network	CurrentVer sion\Polici es\ System\Le galNoticeC aption
Number of previous logons to cache	0	0	MACHINE \Software\ Microsoft\ Windows NT\Current Version\ Winlogon\ CachedLog onsCount
Require domain controller authentication to unlock workstation	Enabled	Enabled	MACHINE \Software\ Microsoft\ Windows NT\Current Version\ Winlogon\ ForceUnlo ckLogon
Require smart cards	Dependent on your risk assessment and	Default	

Parameter	Secure server settings	Normal server settings	Registry setting
	subsequent requirements		
Smart card removal behavior	Lock workstation	Lock workstation	MACHINE \Software\ Microsoft\ Windows NT\Current Version\ Winlogon\ ScRemove Option
Amount of idle time required before disconnecting session for Microsoft® Network Server	15 minutes	15 minutes	MACHINE \System\Cu rrentContro lSet\Servic es\LanMan Server\Para meters\Aut oDisconne ct
Digitally sign communicatio ns for Microsoft® Network Server (always)	Enabled	Enabled	MACHINE \System\Cu rrentContro lSet\Servic es\LanMan Server\Para meters\Req uireSecurit

Parameter	Secure server settings	Normal server settings	Registry setting
			ySignature
Digitally sign communicatio ns for Microsoft® Network Server (if client agrees)	Enabled	Enabled	MACHINE \System\Cu rrentContro lSet\Servic es\LanMan Server\Para meters\Ena bleSecurity Signature
Send unencrypted password to third-party SMB servers	Disabled	Disabled	MACHINE \System\Cu rrentContro lSet\Servic es\Lanman Workstatio n\Paramete rs\EnablePl ainTextPas sword
Disconnect clients when logon hours expire	Enabled	Enabled	MACHINE \System\Cu rrentContro lSet\Servic es\LanMan Server\Para meters\Ena bleForcedL

Parameter	Secure server settings	Normal server settings	Registry setting
			ogOff
Enable automatic logon	Disabled	Disabled	MACHINE \Software\ Microsoft\ Windows NT\Current Version\ Winlogon\ AutoAdmi nLogon
IP source routing protection level (protects against packet spoofing)	2	2	MACHINE \System\Cu rrentContro lSet\Servic es\Tcpip\P arameters\ DisableIPS ourceRouti ng
Allow automatic detection of dead network gateways (could lead to a denial of service)	Disabled	Disabled	MACHINE \System\Cu rrentContro lSet\Servic es\Tcpip\P arameters\ EnableDea dGWDetec t

Parameter	Secure server settings	Normal server settings	Registry setting
Allow ICMP redirects to override OSPF generated routes	Disabled	Disabled	MACHINE \System\Cu rrentContro lSet\Servic es\Tcpip\P arameters\ EnableICM PRedirect
Hide computer from the browse list	This should be enabled if you are putting the domain controller in a highly secure environment and your risk assessment supports this requirement	Default	MACHINE \System\Cu rrentContro lSet\Servic es\Lanman server\Para meters\Hid den
How often keep-alive packets are sent in milliseconds	300000 (or 5 minutes)	300000 (or 5 minutes)	MACHINE \System\Cu rrentContro lSet\Servic es\Tcpip\P arameters\ KeepAlive Time
Configure	Enabled	Enabled	MACHINE

Parameter	Secure server settings	Normal server settings	Registry setting
IPsec exemptions for various types of network traffic			\System\CurrentControlSet\Services\IPSEC\NoDefaultExempt
Disable autorun for all drives	Enabled	Enabled	MACHINE\SOFTWARE\Microsoft\Windows\CurrentVersion\Policies\Explorer\NoDriveTypeAutoRun
Allow the computer to ignore NetBIOS name release requests except from WINS servers	1	1	MACHINE\System\CurrentControlSet\Services\Netbt\Parameters\NoNameReleaseOnDemand
Stop the computer	Enabled	Disabled	MACHINE\System\Cu

Parameter	Secure server settings	Normal server settings	Registry setting
generating 8.3 style filenames			rrentContro lSet\Contro l\FileSyste m\NtfsDisa ble8dot3Na meCreation
Allow IRDP to detect and configure default gateway addresses (could lead to a denial of service)	0	Disabled	MACHINE \System\Cu rrentContro lSet\Servic es\Tcpip\P arameters\ PerformRo uterDiscov ery
Enable safe DLL search mode	Enabled	Enabled	MACHINE \SYSTEM\ CurrentCo ntrol Set\Control \Session Manager\ SafeDllSea rchMode
The time in seconds before the screensaver	0	0	MACHINE \SYSTEM\ Software\ Microsoft\

Parameter	Secure server settings	Normal server settings	Registry setting
grace period expires			Windows NT\ CurrentVer sion\Winlo gon\ ScreenSave rGracePeri od
Syn attack protection level (protects against denial of service)	2	2	MACHINE \System\Cu rrentContro lSet\Servic es\Tcpip\P arameters\ SynAttack Protect
SYN-ACK retransmission s when a connection request is not acknowledged	0	0	MACHINE \System\Cu rrentContro lSet\Servic es\Tcpip\P arameters\ TcpMaxCo nnectRespo nseRetrans missions
How many times	3	3	MACHINE \System\Cu

Parameter	Secure server settings	Normal server settings	Registry setting
unacknowledged data is retransmitted			rrentContro lSet\Servic es\Tcpip\P arameters\ TcpMaxDa taRetransm issions
Percentage threshold for the security event log at which the system will generate a warning	90%	90%	MACHINE \SYSTEM\ CurrentCo ntrol Set\Service s\Eventlog\ Security\ WarningLe vel
Allow anonymous SID/Name translation	Disabled	Disabled	N/A
Do not allow anonymous enumeration of SAM accounts	Enabled	Enabled	MACHINE \System\Cu rrentContro lSet\Contro l\Lsa\Restri ctAnonym ousSAM
Do not allow	Enabled	Enabled	MACHINE

Parameter	Secure server settings	Normal server settings	Registry setting
anonymous enumeration of SAM accounts and shares			\System\Cu rrentContro lSet\Contro l\Lsa\Restri ctAnonym ous
Do not allow storage of credentials or .NET passports for network authentication	Enabled	Enabled	MACHINE \System\Cu rrentContro lSet\Contro l\Lsa\Disab leDomainC reds
Let Everyone permissions apply to anonymous users	Disabled	Disabled	MACHINE \System\Cu rrentContro lSet\Contro l\Lsa\Every oneInclude s Anonymou s
Named pipes that can be accessed anonymously	None	Default	MACHINE \System\Cu rrentContro lSet\Servic es\LanMan Server\Para

Parameter	Secure server settings	Normal server settings	Registry setting
			meters\Nul lSessionPip es
Remotely accessible registry paths and subpaths	System\ CurrentContro lSet\Control\Pr int\ Printers System\ CurrentContro lSet\Services\ Eventlog Software\ Microsoft\OL AP Server Software\ Microsoft\ Windows NT\ CurrentVersio n\ Print Software\ Microsoft\Win dows NT\ CurrentVersio n\ Windows System\ CurrentContro l		MACHINE \System\Cu rrentContro lSet\Contro l\SecurePip eServers\W inreg\Allo wedPaths\ Machine

Parameter	Secure server settings	Normal server settings	Registry setting
	lSet\ContentIndex System\CurrentControlSet\Control\Terminal Server System\CurrentControlSet\Control\Terminal Server\UserConfig System\CurrentControlSet\Control\Terminal Server\Default UserConfiguration Software\Microsoft\Windows NT\CurrentVersion\perflib System\CurrentControlSet\Services\SysmonLog		

Parameter	Secure server settings	Normal server settings	Registry setting
Restrict anonymous access to named shares and pipes	Enabled	Enabled	MACHINE \System\Cu rrentContro lSet\Servic es\LanMan Server\Para meters\Res trictNullSe ssAccess
Shares that can be accessed anonymously	None	None	MACHINE \System\Cu rrentContro lSet\Servic es\LanMan Server\Para meters\Nul lSessionSh ares
Sharing and security model for local accounts	Classic	Classic	MACHINE \System\Cu rrentContro lSet\Contro l\Lsa\Force Guest
Do not store LAN Manager hash value on next password	Enabled	Enabled	MACHINE \System\Cu rrentContro lSet\Contro

Parameter	Secure server settings	Normal server settings	Registry setting
change			l\Lsa\NoL MHash
LAN Manager authentication level	Send NTLMv2, refuse LM and NTLM	Send NTLMv2, refuse LM	MACHINE \System\Cu rrentContro lSet\Contro l\Lsa\LmC ompatibilit yLevel
LDAP client signing requirements	Negotiate signing or require signing	Negotiate signing	MACHINE \System\Cu rrentContro lSet\Servic es\LDAP\L DAPClient Integrity
Minimum session security for NTLM SSP-based (including secure RPC) clients	Require message integrity, message confidentiality, NTLMv2 session security, 128-bit encryption	Require NTLMv2 session security, 128-bit encryption	MACHINE \System\Cu rrentContro lSet\Contro l\Lsa\MSV 1_0\NTLM Min ClientSec
Minimum session security for	Require message integrity,	Require NTLMv2 session	MACHINE \System\Cu rrentContro

Parameter	Secure server settings	Normal server settings	Registry setting
NTLM SSP-based (including secure RPC) servers	message confidentiality, NTLMv2 session security, 128-bit encryption	security, 128-bit encryption	lSet\Contro l\Lsa\MSV 1_0\NTLM Min ServerSec
Allow automatic administrative logon as part of recovery console	Disabled	Disabled	MACHINE \Software\ Microsoft\ Windows NT\Current Version\Se tup\ RecoveryC onsole\Sec urityLevel
Allow floppy copy and access to all drives and all folders for recovery console	Disabled	Default	MACHINE \Software\ Microsoft\ Windows NT\Current Version\Se tup\ RecoveryC onsole\Set Command
Allow system to be shut	Disabled	Disabled	MACHINE \Software\

Parameter	Secure server settings	Normal server settings	Registry setting
down without having to log on			Microsoft\ Windows\ CurrentVer sion\Polici es\ System\Sh utdownWit houtLogon
Clear virtual memory page file	Enabled	Enabled	MACHINE \System\Cu rrentContro lSet\Contro l\Session Manager\ Memory Manageme nt\ClearPa geFileAtSh ut down
Force strong key protection for user keys stored on the computer	User must enter a password each time they use a key	User is prompted when the key is first used	
Use FIPS-compliant algorithms for	Enabled	Disabled	MACHINE \System\Cu rrentContro

Parameter	Secure server settings	Normal server settings	Registry setting
encryption, hashing, and signing			lSet\Control\Lsa\FIPS Algorithm Policy
Require case insensitivity for non-Windows® subsystems	Enabled	Enabled	MACHINE\System\CurrentControlSet\Control\Session Manager\Kernel\ObCaseInsensitive
Strengthen default permissions of internal system objects	Enabled	Enabled	MACHINE\System\CurrentControlSet\Control\Session Manager\Protection Mode
Optional subsystems	None	None	MACHINE\System\CurrentControlSet\Control\Session Manager\SubSystem

Parameter	Secure server settings	Normal server settings	Registry setting
			s\Optional
Use certificate rules on Windows® executables for software restriction policies	Enabled	Default	
Admin approval mode for the built-in Administrator account	Enabled	Enabled	MACHINE \Software\ Microsoft\ Windows\ CurrentVer sion\Polici es\ System\Filt erAdminist ratorToken
Allow UIAccess applications to prompt for elevation without using the secure desktop	Disabled	Disabled	
Behavior of the elevation	Prompt for credentials	Prompt for credentials	MACHINE \Software\

Parameter	Secure server settings	Normal server settings	Registry setting
prompt for administrators in Admin Approval mode			Microsoft\ Windows\ CurrentVer sion\Polici es\ System\Co nsentProm ptBehavior Admin
Behavior of the elevation prompt for standard users	Automatically deny elevation requests	Automatically deny elevation requests	MACHINE \Software\ Microsoft\ Windows\ CurrentVer sion\Polici es\ System\Co nsentProm ptBehavior User
Detect application installations and prompt for elevation	Enabled	Enabled	MACHINE \Software\ Microsoft\ Windows\ CurrentVer sion\Polici es\ System\En ableInstalle

Parameter	Secure server settings	Normal server settings	Registry setting
			rDetection
Only elevate executables that are signed and validated	Disabled	Disabled	MACHINE \Software\ Microsoft\ Windows\ CurrentVer sion\Polici es\ System\Val idateAdmi nCode Signatures
Only elevate UIAccess applications that are installed in secure locations	Enabled	Enabled	MACHINE \Software\ Microsoft\ Windows\ CurrentVer sion\Polici es\ System\En ableSecure UIAPaths
Run all administrators in Admin Approval mode	Enabled	Enabled	MACHINE \Software\ Microsoft\ Windows\ CurrentVer sion\Polici

Parameter	Secure server settings	Normal server settings	Registry setting
			es\ System\En ableLUA
Switch to the secure desktop when prompting for elevation	Enabled	Enabled	MACHINE \Software\ Microsoft\ Windows\ CurrentVer sion\Polici es\ System\Pro mptOnSec ureDesktop
Virtualize file and registry write failures to per-user locations	Enabled	Enabled	MACHINE \Software\ Microsoft\ Windows\ CurrentVer sion\Polici es\ System\En ableVirtual ization

Securing Windows® services

For Windows® services the following permissions should be set:

- Administrators = Full control
- System = Full control
- Interactive = Read.

Table 63: Windows® service settings

Service	Secure server setting	Normal server setting
Active Directory® Domain Services	Automatic	Default
Active Directory® Certificate Services	Automatic	
Adrmsloggingservice	Default	Default
AeLookupSvc	Automatic	Default
Application Host Helper Service	Default	Default
Application Information	Manual	Default
Application Layer Gateway Service	Manual	Default
Application Management	Manual	Default
Background Intelligent Transfer Service	Automatic	Automatic
Base Filtering Engine	Automatic	Automatic

Service	Secure server setting	Normal server setting
Certificate Propagation	Manual	Automatic
CNG Key Isolation	Manual	Default
COM+ Event System	Automatic	Automatic
COM+ System Application	Manual	Default
Computer Browser	Disabled	Default
Cryptographic Services	Automatic	Automatic
DCOM Server Process Launcher	Automatic	Automatic
Desktop Window Manager Session Manager	Automatic	Automatic
DFS Namespace	Automatic	Default
DFS Replication	Automatic	Default
DHCP Client	Automatic	Automatic
DHCP Server	Automatic	Default
Diagnostic Policy Service	Automatic	Default
Diagnostic Service Host	Manual	Default
Diagnostic System Host	Manual	Default
Distributed Link Tracking	Automatic	Default

Service	Secure server setting	Normal server setting
Client		
Distributed Transaction Coordinator	Automatic	Default
DNS Client	Automatic	Default
DNS Server	Automatic	Default
Extensible Authentication Protocol	Manual	Default
Fax	Disabled	Default
Function Discovery Provider Host	Manual	Default
Function Discovery Resource Publication	Manual	Default
Group Policy Client	Automatic	Automatic
Health Key and Certificate Management	Manual	Default
Human Interface Device Access	Manual	Default
IKE and AuthIP IPsec Keying Modules	Automatic	Automatic
Interactive Services Detection	Manual	Default
Intersite Messaging	Automatic	Default
Internet Connection Sharing (ICS)	Disabled	Default

Service	Secure server setting	Normal server setting
IP Helper	Automatic	Automatic
IPsec Policy Agent	Automatic	Default
Kerberos Key Distribution Center	Automatic	Default
KtmRm for Distributed Transaction Coordinator	Automatic	Default
Link-Layer Topology Discovery Mapper	Manual	Default
LiveUpdate	Manual	Default
Microsoft .NET Framework NGEN v2.0.50727_X86	Manual	Default
Microsoft Fibre Channel Platform Registration Service	Manual	Automatic
Microsoft iSCSI Initiator Service	Manual	Default
Microsoft Software Shadow Copy Provider	Manual	Default
Multimedia Class Scheduler	Manual	Default
Netlogon	Manual	Default
Network Access Protection Agent	Manual	Default
Network Connections	Manual	Default

Service	Secure server setting	Normal server setting
Network List Service	Automatic	Automatic
Network Location Awareness	Automatic	Automatic
Network Policy Server	Automatic	Default
Network Store Interface Service	Automatic	Automatic
Offline Files	Disabled	Default
Performance Logs & Alerts	Manual	Default
Plug and Play	Automatic	Automatic
PnP-X IP Bus Enumerator	Disabled	Default
Portable Device Enumerator Service	Manual	Default
Print Spooler	Enabled for Print Servers Otherwise Disabled	Default
Problem Reports and Solutions Control Panel Support	Manual	Default
Protected Storage	Manual	Default
Remote Access Auto Connection Manager	Manual	Default
Remote Access	Manual	Default

Service	Secure server setting	Normal server setting
Connection Manager		
Remote Procedure Call (RPC)	Automatic	Automatic
Remote Procedure Call (RPC) Locator	Manual	Default
Remote Registry	Manual	Automatic
Resultant Set of Policy Provider	Manual	Default
Routing and Remote Access	Disabled	Default
SavRoam	Manual	Default
Secondary Logon	Automatic	Default
Secure Socket Tunneling Protocol Service	Manual	Default
Security Accounts Manager	Automatic	Automatic
Server	Automatic	Automatic
Shell Hardware Detection	Automatic	Automatic
SL UI Notification Service	Manual	Default
Smart Card	Manual	Automatic
Smart Card Removal Policy	Manual	Default

Service	Secure server setting	Normal server setting
SNMP Trap	Manual	Default
Software Licensing	Automatic	Automatic
Special Administration Console Helper	Manual	Default
SSDP Discovery	Disabled	Default
Superfetch	Disabled	Default
System Event Notification Service	Automatic	Default
Task Scheduler	Automatic	Automatic
TCP/IP NetBIOS Helper	Automatic	Automatic
Telephony	Manual	Default
Terminal Server	Automatic	Default
Terminal Services Configuration	Manual	Default
Terminal Services UserMode Port Redirector	Manual	Default
Themes	Disabled	Default
Thread Ordering Server	Manual	Default
TPM Base Services	Automatic	Default

Service	Secure server setting	Normal server setting
UPnP Device Host	Disabled	Default
User Profile Service	Automatic	Automatic
Virtual Disk	Manual	Default
Virtual Machine Additions Services Application	Automatic	Default
Virtual Machine Additions Shared Folder Service	Automatic	Default
Volume Shadow Copy	Manual	Default
Windows® Audio	Manual	Default
Windows® Audio Endpoint Builder	Manual	Default
Windows® Color System	Manual	Default
Windows® Driver Foundation - User-mode Driver Framework	Manual	Default
Windows® Error Reporting Service	Automatic	Default
Windows® Event Collector	Manual	Default
Windows® Event Log	Automatic	Automatic
Windows® Firewall	Automatic	Automatic
Windows® Installer	Manual	Default

Service	Secure server setting	Normal server setting
Windows® Management Instrumentation	Automatic	Automatic
Windows® Modules Installer	Manual	Default
Windows® Remote Management (WS-Management)	Automatic	Default
Windows® Time	Automatic	Automatic
Windows® Update	Automatic	Automatic
WinHTTP Web Proxy Auto-Discovery Service	Manual	Default
Wired AutoConfig	Manual	Default
WMI Performance Adapter	Manual	Default
Workstation	Automatic	Default

Table 64: Securing user rights

Parameter	Secure server settings	Normal server settings
Access credential manager as a trusted caller	No one	Default
Access this computer from the network	Administrators Authenticated Users	Administrators Authenticated Users

Parameter	Secure server settings	Normal server settings
	Enterprise Domain Controllers	
Act as part of the operating system	No one	No one
Add workstations to the domain	Administrators	Default
Adjust memory quota for a process	Administrators Network Service Local Service	Default
Allow to log on locally	Administrators	Administrators
Allow to log on through terminal services	Administrators	Administrators
Back up files and directories	Administrators Backup Operators	Default
Bypass traverse tracking	Authenticated Users Local Service Network Service	Administrators Authenticated Users Backup Operators Local Service Network Service
Change the system time	Administrators Local Service	Administrators Local Service

Parameter	Secure server settings	Normal server settings
Create a pagefile	Administrators Local Service	Administrators
Create a token object	No one	Default
Create global objects	Administrators Network Service Local Service SERVICE	Default
Create permanent shared objects	No one	Default
Create symbolic links	Administrators	Default
Debug programs	No one	Administrators
Deny access to this computer from the network (minimum)	Guest	Guest
Deny logon as a batch job	Guest	Guest
Deny logon as a service	No one	Default
Deny logon locally	Guests	Guests
Deny logon through terminal services (minimum)	Guests	Guests
Enable computer and user accounts to be	Administrators	Default

Parameter	Secure server settings	Normal server settings
trusted for delegation		
Force shutdown from a remote system	Administrators	Default
Generate security audits	Local Service Network Service	Local Service Network Service
Impersonate client after authentication	Administrators Network Service Local Service SERVICE	Default
Increase a process working set	Administrators Local Service	Default
Increase scheduling priority	Administrator	Default
Load and unload device drivers	Administrator	Default
Lock pages in memory	No one	Default
Log on as a batch job	Administrators	Default
Log on as a service	Administrators	Default
Manage audit and security logs	Administrators	Administrators
Modify firmware environment values	Administrators	Administrators

Parameter	Secure server settings	Normal server settings
Perform volume maintenance tasks	Administrators	Default
Profile single process	Administrators	Administrators
Profile system performance	Administrators	Administrators
Remove computer from docking station	Administrators	Administrators
Replace a process level token	Network Service Local Service	Network Service Local Service
Restore files and directories	Administrators Backup Operators	Administrators Backup Operators
Shut down the system	Administrator	Administrator Backup Operators
Synchronise Directory Service data	No one	Default
Take ownership of file or other object	Administrator	Administrator

Setting file system permissions

Note that, unless stated otherwise, Administrator and/or System full control is for the designated folder and all its contents.

Table 65: File system permissions

Parameter	Secure server settings	Normal server settings
%SystemDrive% e.g. C:	Administrators = Full System = Full Creator Owner = Full Interactive = Read, Execute	Default
%SystemRoot%\system32\at.exe	Administrators = Full System =Full	Administrators = Full System =Full
%SystemRoot%\system32\attrib.exe	Administrators = Full System =Full	Administrators = Full System =Full
%SystemRoot%\system32\cacls.exe	Administrators = Full System =Full	Administrators = Full System =Full
%SystemRoot%\system32\debug.exe	Administrators = Full System =Full	Administrators = Full System =Full

Parameter	Secure server settings	Normal server settings
%SystemRoot%\system32\drwatson. exe	Administrators = Full System =Full	Administrators = Full System =Full
%SystemRoot%\system32\drwtsn32. exe	Administrators = Full System =Full	Administrators = Full System =Full
%SystemRoot%\system32\edlin.exe	Administrators = Full System =Full Interactive=Full	Administrators = Full System =Full Interactive=Full
%SystemRoot%\system32\eventcrea te	Administrators = Full System =Full	Administrators = Full System =Full
SystemRoot%\system32\eventtrigger s.exe	Administrators = Full System =Full	Administrators = Full System =Full
%SystemRoot%\system32\ftp.exe	Administrators = Full System =Full Interactive=Full	Administrators = Full System =Full Interactive=Full
%SystemRoot%\system32\net.exe	Administrators = Full System =Full	Administrators = Full System =Full

Parameter	Secure server settings	Normal server settings
	Interactive=Full	Interactive=Full
%SystemRoot%\system32\net1.exe	Administrators = Full System =Full Interactive=Full	Administrators = Full System =Full Interactive=Full
%SystemRoot%\system32\netsh.exe	Administrators = Full System =Full	Administrators = Full System =Full
%SystemRoot%\system32\rcp.exe	Administrators = Full System =Full	Administrators = Full System =Full
%SystemRoot%\system32\reg.exe	Administrators = Full System =Full	Administrators = Full System =Full
%SystemRoot%\regedit.exe	Administrators = Full System =Full	Administrators = Full System =Full
%SystemRoot%\system32\regedt32. exe	Administrators = Full System =Full	Administrators = Full System =Full
%SystemRoot%\system32\regsvr32. exe	Administrators = Full	Administrators = Full

Parameter	Secure server settings	Normal server settings
	System =Full	System =Full
%SystemRoot%\system32\rexec.exe	Administrators = Full System =Full	Administrators = Full System =Full
%SystemRoot%\system32\rsh.exe	Administrators = Full System =Full	Administrators = Full System =Full
%SystemRoot%\system32\runas.exe	Administrators = Full System =Full Interactive=Full	Administrators = Full System =Full Interactive=Full
%SystemRoot%\system32\sc.exe	Administrators = Full System =Full	Administrators = Full System =Full
%SystemRoot%\system32\subst.exe	Administrators = Full System =Full	Administrators = Full System =Full
%SystemRoot%\system32\telnet.exe	Administrators = Full System =Full Interactive=Full	Administrators = Full System =Full Interactive=Full

Parameter	Secure server settings	Normal server settings
%SystemRoot%\system32\tftp.exe	Administrators = Full System =Full Interactive=Full	Administrators = Full System =Full Interactive=Full
%SystemRoot%\system32\tlntsvr.exe	Administrators = Full System =Full	Administrators = Full System =Full

Configuring registry permissions

Note that unless stated otherwise:

- Administrators or System full control is full control for the designated key and all subkeys.
- Creator Owner full control is for subkeys only.
- Users' permissions are for current key, subkeys and values.

Table 66: Registry permissions

Parameter	Secure server settings	Normal server settings
HKLM\Software	Administrator = Full System = Full Creator Owner = Full Users = Read	Administrator = Full System = Full Creator Owner = Full Users = Read

Parameter	Secure server settings	Normal server settings
HKLM\Software\Microsoft\Windows\CurrentVersion\Installer	Administrator = Full System = Full Users = Read	Administrator = Full System = Full Users = Read
HKLM\Software\Microsoft\Windows\CurrentVersion\Policies	Administrator = Full System = Full Creator Owner = Full Authenticated Users = Read	Administrator = Full System = Full Creator Owner = Full Authenticated Users = Read
HKLM\System	Administrator = Full System = Full Creator Owner = Full Users = Read	Administrator = Full System = Full Creator Owner = Full Users = Read
HKLM\System\CurrentControlSet\Enum	Administrator = Full System = Full Authenticated Users = Read	Administrator = Full System = Full Authenticated Users = Read
HKLM\System\CurrentControlSet\Services\SNMP\Parameters\PermittedManagers	Administrator = Full System = Full Creator Owner = Full	Administrator = Full System = Full Creator Owner = Full

Parameter	Secure server settings	Normal server settings
HKLM\System\CurrentControlSet\Services\SNMP\Parameters\ValidCommunities	Administrator = Full System = Full Creator Owner = Full	Administrator = Full System = Full Creator Owner = Full
HKLM\Software\Microsoft\MSDTC	Administrator = Full System = Full Network Service = Query Value, Set Value, Create subkey, Enumerate subkeys, Notify, Read permissions, Users = Read	Administrator = Full System = Full Network Service = Query Value, Set Value, Create subkey, Enumerate subkeys, Notify, Read permissions, Users = Read
HKU\Default\Software\Microsoft\System Certificates\Root\ProtectedRoots	Administrator = Full System = Full Users = Read	Administrator = Full System = Full Users = Read
KKLM\SOFTWARE\Microsoft\Windows NT\CurrentVersion\SeCEdit	Administrator = Full System = Full Users = Read	Administrator = Full System = Full Users = Read

Protecting files and directories

In order to meet the confidentiality, integrity and availability (CIA) requirements of the ISO27001 information security standard for your information assets, where possible you should store all data on centralised servers to ensure that the data is centrally managed, secured and backed up.

To enforce security on files and file system objects, such as folders, you should ensure that all folders and files to be shared by the Windows Server® 2008 or 2012 servers are located on partitions formatted with the NTFS file system. With the NTFS file system you can set the appropriate permissions on each directory/folder depending on the data owner's requirements.

In addition, and if your risk assessment indicates the need for enhanced security for this information, you can employ the Windows Server® 2008 or 2012 BitLocker™ tool to encrypt partitions or folders as required.

You should also ensure that all Windows® 7 or 8 client machines have the NTFS file system installed on their partitions. This will enable users to create secure folders on their hard drives in the event they need to store data on their own computers. If the data is of a sensitive nature or the computer is a portable computer, you can also encrypt the hard drive of the system using the BitLocker™ facility that is built into Microsoft® Windows® 7 and 8.

APPENDIX 1: OVERVIEW OF SECURITY SETTINGS FOR WINDOWS SERVER® 2008 AND 2012 SERVERS AND DOMAIN CONTROLLERS

This appendix explains each of the settings identified in Chapters 9 to 11 and provides explanations for why the recommended settings are necessary if you are to effectively secure the Microsoft environment.

Service pack and hotfixes

Current service pack installed

Microsoft distributes large updates to its operating system that contain all major and minor bugfixes and, in some cases, enhancements to the operating system. At the time of writing,[49] the service pack currently available for Microsoft® Windows Server® 2008 is Service Pack 2. Microsoft completes extensive testing on the service pack prior to release. However, you should ensure that all service packs are extensively tested on your own test systems before applying them to your production systems. Ideally, you should also wait a number of weeks after the service pack is released and monitor bug reports for any potential (new) issues with it.

Note that Microsoft also releases service packs for various Microsoft applications, such as Internet Explorer®, Microsoft® Exchange, and Microsoft® SQL Server®. These

---

[49] May 2014.

service packs should also be tested and installed as with operating system service packs.

Latest update rollup installed

Microsoft® Windows Server® 2012 releases the same updates through 'update rollups'. These updates are released more regularly, and generally comprise smaller individual patches and modifications than those contained in the Microsoft® Windows Server® 2008 service packs. The most recent update rollup at the time of writing[50] is April 2013.

Just as you should extensively test service packs on your own test systems before applying them to your production systems, so too should you test update rollups. You should also wait a number of weeks after the update rollup is released and monitor bug reports for any potential (new) issues with it.

Software patches

Patches are minor software releases published by Microsoft to address specific bugs or issues with their products. Patches are tested by Microsoft but only in so far as ensuring the patch addresses a specific issue. Patches do not undergo the same rigorous testing as service packs. Therefore they should be tested thoroughly before being implemented on your production systems.

---

[50] May 2014.

Account and audit policies

Account policies

Minimum password length

Specifying the minimum password length prevents users from creating simple passwords that are easy to guess. It will prevent potential attackers from accessing the system either by using password-guessing techniques or using automated utilities to guess the passwords using a brute force attack. A brute force attack is an automated attack where all combinations of all characters are very rapidly entered into the system in an attempt to identify the password.

Having long passwords makes it harder for an attacker to guess the password and also makes the process of a brute force attack longer. Making the process longer makes it easier to detect a potential attack on the network.

In addition to the above password-guessing attacks, some legacy Microsoft authentication protocols, such as LAN Manager (LANMan) and NTLM, suffer from a limitation which makes an eight-character password particularly important[51]. These protocols effectively break down passwords into seven-character 'chunks'. This means that passwords with seven or fewer characters are easy to guess and identify.

---

[51] Microsoft now discourages the use of NTLM in applications due to a lack of support for more recent cryptographic methods. *http://msdn.microsoft.com/en-us/library/cc236715.aspx*.

Appendix 1: Overview of Security Settings for Windows Server® 2008 Servers and Domain Controllers

General industry consensus now agrees that eight-character passwords should be the minimum password length. In addition, stronger authentication protocols should be employed on the network, such as NTLMv2 or Kerberos.

Maximum password age

All passwords must be changed regularly to ensure a password is known only to the user authorised to use that particular account. Having passwords expire regularly forces users to change their passwords accordingly. Once a password's age reaches this parameter, the user will be made to change it.

This also ensures that passwords for old accounts that have not been deleted or managed properly will expire and will not be easily compromised.

Minimum password age

To prevent users quickly changing their password back to a previous one, the minimum password age ensures the password must be in existence for a certain number of days before it can be changed.

Password complexity

Using passwords that are all numeric or alpha characters makes them easy to guess and easy to crack using a brute force attack. Employing password complexity ensures that users employ a combination of numeric, upper and lower case alpha, and special characters, thus making the passwords difficult to guess.

Password history

A weakness in user password management is created when users regularly employ the same passwords. Retaining a password history prevents users from doing this.

Store passwords using reversible encryption

This setting is disabled by default. Windows Server® 2008 and 2012 uses hashing techniques to protect passwords. This prevents the passwords from being easily read. However, some legacy applications may require that passwords can be reversibly decrypted. This setting must be enabled with great care.

Audit policy

Auditing significant system events on servers provides a means of being alerted to critical events as they happen, thereby enabling a rapid response. Auditing also provides a historical view of what happened so that incidents can be investigated.

Account logon events: Auditing account logon events monitors access to the server from domain accounts. A high failure rate of account logons could indicate a password-guessing attack.

Account management: Tracking account management events ensures that all attempts to create, modify or delete accounts are recorded. This is important when investigating alterations to accounts, rogue account set-ups/deletions or determining why an account was locked out.

Logon events: Auditing logon events ensures that local account access to the server is monitored. This includes accounts, such as the Local Administrator account, machine accounts and/or services accounts.

Object access: Auditing object access allows user access to specific resources, such as printers, files or folders to be monitored regularly. Note that this setting can create a large number of events in the event log, depending on the number of objects being audited.

Policy changes: This setting will ensure that all changes to user rights, account policies, group policies, etc. will be recorded.

System events: Auditing system events will ensure that items, such as starting and restarting the server, starting and restarting services and other system events are auditable.

Directory service access: Directory service access auditing tracks access to objects within Active Directory®. This requires specific objects to have system access control lists configured for auditing. Note that this can create a large number of events in the log entries.

Privilege use: This setting enables auditing for any operation that would require a user account to make use of extra privileges that it had already been assigned. Therefore accounts with extra privileges, such as Backup Operators, will generate a lot of events in the event log. Typically this setting is enabled when investigating rogue activity on the system or by a specific account.

Process tracking: Auditing process tracking is rarely used as it generates a lot of events in the system logs whenever users start, stop or otherwise changes a process. As with the privilege use option, this setting should only be enabled when investigating issues with the system.

Account lockout policy

The account lockout policy will prevent passwords from being continuously guessed while the user is online, e.g. dialling in remotely.

Account lockout threshold: This setting determines how many times the user is allowed to incorrectly enter their account credentials before being automatically locked out.

Lockout after: If a user attempts to log in the number of times specified in this parameter and fails to do so, their account will be logged out and they will be unable to log in to the domain.

Reset count after: This setting is used in conjunction with the account lockout threshold value. The counter for bad logon attempts is cleared and reset to zero after the specified time within this parameter. The value in this parameter should be less than or equal to that specified in the 'lockout duration' value.

Lockout duration: One the criteria for account lockout have been met, the duration that the account remains locked out can be set. Setting this value to zero means the account is locked out until the administrator resets it. This prevents automatic password-guessing attacks from targeting a specific address. Note, however, that an attacker can exploit this feature to cause a denial-of-service attack by locking out all accounts.

Forcibly disconnect remote user from server when logon hours expire: Domain accounts may be limited to specific hours when they may be used. By default, the domain controller only enforces these settings upon logon, but not after the session is established. With this setting enabled, the user's network connections will be closed when their allotted time has been reached.

Event log settings

Windows Server® 2008 and 2012 record critical events in a variety of event logs:

- Application logs record the activities of applications on the server.
- Security logs record all security and auditing events.
- System logs record operating-system events.

Application log settings

Maximum event log size: The default log size is 512 KB. However, to ensure that all events are properly recorded, this setting should be increased to an appropriate size.

Restrict guest access: As the event log contains important information, it should not be available to guest accounts.

Log retention method: This determines how the operating system manages system logs that are full. There are three options:

- Overwrite events as needed: continues writing events to the logs and overwrites old events as needed. This could allow an attacker to cover their tracks by deliberately filling the event logs.

- Overwrite by days: specify how many days the system retains the event logs before overwriting them. Events older than a specific number of days will be overwritten.
- Do not overwrite (clear logs manually): do not overwrite any events until the logs have been cleared manually by the administrator or an automated log management system.

Log retention: This determines the number of days the logs will be kept in conjunction with the log retention method being set to 'overwrite by days'.

Security log settings

Maximum event log size: The default log size is 512 KB. However, to ensure that all events are properly recorded, this setting should be increased to an appropriate size.

Restrict guest access: As the event log contains important information, it should not be available to guest accounts.

Log retention method: This determines how the operating system manages system logs that are full. There are three options:

- Overwrite events as needed: continues writing events to the logs and overwrites old events as needed. This could allow an attacker to cover their tracks by deliberately filling the event logs.
- Overwrite by days: specify how many days the system retains the event logs before overwriting them. Events older than a specific number of days will be overwritten.
- Do not overwrite (clear logs manually): do not overwrite any events until the logs have been cleared manually by

the administrator or an automated log management system.

Log retention: Determines the number of days the logs will be kept in conjunction with the log retention method being set to 'overwrite by days'.

System log settings

Maximum event log size: The default log size is 512 KB. However, to ensure that all events are properly recorded, this setting should be increased to an appropriate size.

Restrict guest access: As the event log contains important information, it should not be available to guest accounts.

Log retention method: This determines how the operating system manages system logs that are full. There are three options:

- Overwrite events as needed: continues writing events to the logs and overwrites old events as needed. This could allow an attacker to cover their tracks by deliberately filling the event logs.
- Overwrite by days: specify how many days the system retains the event logs before overwriting them. Events older than a specific number of days will be overwritten.
- Do not overwrite (clear logs manually): do not overwrite any events until the logs have been cleared manually by the administrator or an automated log management system.

Log retention: Determines the number of days the logs will be kept in conjunction with the log retention method being set to 'overwrite by days'.

Security settings

Allow anonymous SID/Name translation

Each object in the Active Directory® is recognised by the system in the form of a binary identity number known as a SID. The formatting of SIDs and their structure is well known and it is therefore easy for an attacker to identify which accounts are administrator accounts by their associated SIDS. Disabling this setting prevents an anonymous or null user from translating the SID into an account name.

Do not allow anonymous enumeration of SAM accounts

All user names in the domain account database (SAM) can be remotely identified by an attacker using an anonymous or null account. Enabling this setting prevents this from occurring.

Do not allow anonymous enumeration of SAM accounts and shares

In addition to preventing null users from seeing the domain account database, this setting also prevents the null attacker from determining what shares are available on the network. Note that there is no recommendation on whether this setting should be used in conjunction with or instead of 'do not allow anonymous enumeration of SAM accounts'; best practice recommends that both settings be set to 'enabled'.

Appendix 1: Overview of Security Settings for Windows Server® 2008 Servers and Domain Controllers

Administrator account status

The administrator account is the one account that is common to all Microsoft® Windows® installations in the world. This account also has the most privileges in the domain. This means that a potential attacker can attack the network by trying to guess the password for the administrator account. As this account is never locked out, it provides a means of attack on the network. Disabling the administrator account prevents an attack using the account named 'administrator'.

Guest account status

This account is disabled by default. If enabled, it can provide an avenue of attack to the network and therefore should remain disabled at all times.

Limit local account use of blank passwords to console only

Although no passwords should be blank, this setting ensures that no remote user can log on to the server(s) using a local account, in the local accounts database held on the server, that has a blank password.

Rename administrator account

Renaming the administrator account prevents a potential attacker from exploiting that account. This setting should be used in conjunction with the anonymous security identifier (SID)/Name translation setting, which should be disabled.

Rename guest account

For similar reasons to the renaming of the administrator account, the guest account should also be renamed.

Audit the access of global system objects

Enabling this setting will create a large number of events in the system logs. This feature is typically only used by developers trying to identify how their application interacts with the operating system. Therefore this feature should not normally be used.

Audit the use of back-up and restore privileges

Enabling this setting will record all back-up and restore operations for every object. This will create excessive log-file entries.

Shut down system immediately if unable to log security events

In the event that the security log becomes full, the system will be halted until the log files are manually cleared by an administrator.

Allowed to format and eject removable media

This setting governs the types of user which have authority to remove NTFS-formatted media from the computer. The available choices (listed from most to least restrictive) are administrators, administrators and power users, or administrators and interactive users.

Prevent users from installing print drivers

Preventing users from installing print drivers ensures that only authorised devices and their associated drivers are installed on to the system. While this means that only administrators can install printers and may mean additional support calls, it ensures that only proper and validated device drivers are installed on the network.

Restrict CD-ROM access to locally logged-on users only

This setting prevents remote users from accessing CD-ROMS stored in the CD drives of the server. Note that enabling this setting may cause issues with the Windows® Installer service using Microsoft® Installer (.msi) files. The setting can be disabled while the installation of the software is being performed.

Restrict floppy disk access to locally logged-on users only

This setting prevents remote users from accessing files stored on the server's local floppy disk. As sensitive information could be stored on floppy disks used on servers, this setting should be enabled.

Unsigned device driver behavior

Microsoft generally ships drivers with a digital signature, expressing that Microsoft itself has certified the drivers through their Windows® Hardware Quality Lab. Unfortunately, not all drivers (even from Microsoft) have digital signatures.

Options for this setting are:

- Silently succeed: this setting allows the driver to be installed without any notification to the user.
- Warn but allow installation: this provides a message to the user, warning them that the driver is not signed.
- Do not allow installation: prevents the driver from being installed.

Allow server operators to schedule tasks

This setting only applies to domain controllers and prevents operators from adding tasks to the scheduling subsystem.

LDAP server signing requirements

While changing this setting to 'require signing' does not protect the confidentiality of the data in transit, it prevents man-in-the-middle attacks from occurring.

Refuse Machine account password changes

This setting will allow the domain to prevent the computer from changing the computer account password.

Digitally encrypt or sign secure channel data (always)

With this setting enabled, all packets sent from the client will be signed. The client will also encrypt the packets if the server supports it. A signed packet cannot be spoofed or tampered with although the data can be intercepted. Encrypted packets can only be decrypted by the server.

Digitally encrypt secure channel data

As for the previous setting.

Digitally sign secure channel data

By signing secure channel data, this setting will prevent man-in-the-middle attacks.

Disable Machine account password changes

All computers have an account within the domain. These accounts are changed as per normal user accounts. Enabling this setting prevents the workstation from changing its account password. If the local copy of the computer account's password is not the same as that on the domain controller, the machine will have to be added into the domain again.

Maximum Machine account password age

This setting is used in conjunction with the previous setting and determines how often the workstation account password should be changed.

Require strong (Windows® 2000 or later) session key

This option is enabled by default and requires all workstations to use a 128-bit key to encrypt secure channel communications.

Do not display last user name for interactive logon

This setting prevents the user ID used in the last logon session from being displayed on the logon screen.

Do not require Ctrl+Alt+Del

Changing this setting to enabled means that users will not have to press the Ctrl+Alt+Del key sequence to log in. The setting should be set to disabled to ensure users are not entering their logon credentials into an application other than the Windows® logon applications.

Message text for users attempting to log on

Users should be presented with a message or logon banner advising them of the conditions of use of the system before they log in to the system. This should be in line with your security policy. Note that best practice advises not using terms within the message, such as 'Welcome', etc.

Message title for users attempting to log on

This setting is used in conjunction with the previous setting for the logon banner. Note that best practice advises not using terms within the message, such as 'Welcome', etc.

Number of previous logons to cache

Caching logons enables users to log on to workstations when the domain controllers are not available, e.g. for a remote user using a laptop away from the network.

Require domain controller authentication to unlock workstation

This setting can be used to prevent users logging on to the locally cached logon credentials even though the account has been locked out. Without this setting being enabled, the user could continue to attempt to log on to the workstation and succeed against cached logon credentials. Enabling this setting means the users credentials must be confirmed by the domain controller before the user is allowed to log on.

Require smart cards

Enabling this setting allows support for smart card two-factor authentication, which could be used for servers or workstations that contain sensitive information.

Smart card removal behavior

If using smart cards, this setting should be set to 'lock workstation' in the event the smart card is removed from the system.

Amount of idle time required before disconnecting session for Microsoft® Network Server

This setting applies to workstation communications using the SMB protocol. If there has been a defined period of inactivity, the connection with the workstation can be dropped. This frees up resources on the server and blocks a potential channel of attack to the server. The connection is re-established automatically and transparently to the user when communications continue again.

Digitally sign communications for Microsoft® Network Server (always)

This setting can be enabled to require all SMB communications with the server device to be signed.

Digitally sign communications for Microsoft® Network Server (if client agrees)

This option is enabled by default and should remain enabled.

Do not allow storage of credentials or .NET passports for network authentication

This setting controls the behaviour of the 'stored usernames and passwords' feature of Windows®. This feature stores NTLM, Kerberos, Passport and SSL authentication: 'enabled' keeps credentials out of the cache, 'disabled' allows the storing of usernames and passwords.

Note that this setting is separate from the Internet Explorer® authentication cache.

Let Everyone permissions apply to anonymous users

This setting is disabled by default and should remain so. The Everyone group is a special group within Windows Server® 2008 and 2012 and contains all accounts. Enabling this setting allows the Null account to become a member of the Everyone group, thereby increasing its privileges.

Named pipes that can be accessed anonymously

This setting defines which pipes can be accessed remotely without authentication and it should be left blank.

Remotely accessible registry paths

This setting defines the registry paths and corresponding child paths which can be accessed from another computer. It is dependent on the remote registry service and associated authentication lists.

Restrict anonymous access to named shares and pipes

When enabled, the anonymous restrictions on shares and named pipes take effect to prevent null sessions from accessing these resources.

Shares that can be accessed anonymously

Adding specific shares to this list grants access to the unauthenticated null user.

Sharing and security model for local accounts

The classic model allows remote users to log on to the server using local accounts. The guest-only model remaps the remote user to the guest account and they can only access resources available to the guest. Note that this setting should be set to classic in the event that the guest account is inadvertently enabled and granted access to system resources.

Do not store LAN Manager hash value on next password change

This setting prevents the LAN Manager hash from being stored within the SAM database. It should be set to 'enabled'.

LAN Manager authentication level

For historical reasons, Windows Server® 2008 and 2012 support a number of authentication protocols. The original LAN Manager (or LM) password hash is considered very weak, but is still used for backwards compatibility with old Windows® 9x clients. Microsoft® Windows® NT 4.0 provided NTLM authentication, but there are a number of serious vulnerabilities within this protocol. Subsequently, NTLM version 2 (NTLMv2) was introduced. NTLMv2 provides significant improvements to security especially when combined with a strong password policy.

All authentication models work with a hash of the password, not the password itself. This presents challenges with legacy compatibility between operating systems. For interoperability, the default authentication protocol is the basic LM hash together with the more secure NTLM hash.

This setting can be changed to provide a more secure authentication challenge and response mechanism. The options available are:

- Send LM and NTLM responses.
- Send LM and NTLM, use NTLMv2 session security if negotiated.
- Send NTLM response only.
- Send NTLMv2 response only.

- Send NTLMv2 response only\refuse LM.
- Send NTLMv2 response only\refuse LM and NTLM.

Note that in order to ensure backwards compatibility, it may be necessary to use a less-secure authentication protocol.

LDAP client signing requirements

This is similar to the SMB signing requirements discussed earlier in this document and applies to the LDAP protocol accessing the Active Directory®.

Minimum session security for NTLM SSP-based (including secure RPC) clients

NTLM authentication can provide a security service to manage connections between various clients and servers, including through the remote procedure call (RPC) service.

Allow automatic administrative logon as part of recovery console

This setting can bypass the requirement for the local administrator to log on as part of the recovery console process. This would mean any user who could boot the server into the recovery console would gain administrative privileges to the server. This setting should remain at the default of 'disabled'.

Allow floppy copy and access to all drives and all folders for recovery console

By default this setting is disabled and should remain so. This prevents someone from copying data from the hard drive of the server on to removable media when using the recovery console.

Allow system to be shut down without having to log on

This setting should be disabled to prevent servers from being rebooted by unauthorised personnel.

Clear virtual memory page file

The pagefile contains information that was in use within the server's memory. It can potentially hold a great deal of information that is useful for an attacker. Information in the pagefile can reveal SSL web pages, queries sent from the client to databases, sometimes even user IDs and passwords from poorly written applications. By default this setting is disabled and should be enabled for secure servers.

Default owner for objects created by members of the Administrators group

Normally the owner of an object is the creator of the object. This setting allows for all members of the Administrators group to be the owner of an object created by an individual administrator.

Require case insensitivity for non-Windows® subsystems

Enabling this setting allows Windows® to interoperate with case-sensitive operating systems, such as UNIX.

Strengthen default permissions of internal system objects

This should be left at the system default of enabled.

Optional subsystems

Windows® provides default support for the POSIX subsystem, which can provide support for UNIX-like commands. However, badly written subsystem commands can potentially compromise the system. The default 'POSIX' should be changed to 'None' on secure systems unless it is required to support specific subsystem requirements.

Use certificate rules on Windows® executables for software restriction policies

This should be left at the system default of enabled.

(AFD DynamicBacklogGrowthDelta) Number of connections to create when additional connections are necessary for Winsock applications (10 recommended)

Windows® socket applications which support a large number of connections use AFD.sys to manage connection backlogs. Should all the existing connections be used, this setting determines how many additional connections are created. If this is set too large, the computer could be susceptible to a SYN-flood or similar resource-exhaustion attack.

(AFD EnableDynamicBacklog) Enable dynamic backlog for Winsock applications (recommended)

This setting is the overall control for AFD dynamic backlog. When this is set to disable, dynamic backlogging is turned off.

(AFDMaximumDynamicBacklog) Maximum number of 'quasi-free' connections for Winsock applications

A 'quasi-free' connection is one in which the SYN packet is sent, but the full TCP 3-way connection handshake is not yet complete. This setting defines the number of uninitiated and the number of quasi-free connections per listening endpoint.

(AFD MinimumDynamicBacklog) Minimum number of free connections for Winsock applications (20 recommended for systems under attack, 10 otherwise)

This setting defines the minimum number of free connections that can exist before a new thread is created to open up additional connections.

(DisableIPSourceRouting) IP source routing protection level (protects against packet spoofing)

If a Windows® computer has two valid networking devices installed, it can be configured to act as a router or a firewall and pass network traffic from one interface to another, whether this is the intended purpose of the computer or not. 'Source routing' traffic that passes through such a router can bypass certain routing rules by 'spoofing' the device to think malicious network activity came from the protected side.

(EnableDeadGWDetect) Allow automatic detection of dead network gateways (could lead to denial of service)

This setting should be set to '0' (disabled) to prevent an attacker manipulating the default gateway to route network traffic to an alternate address.

(EnableICMPRedirect) Allow ICMP redirects to override OSPF-generated routes

In order to prevent network ICMP traffic from being redirected from one computer to another, set the EnableICMPRedirect value to zero.

(EnablePMTUDiscovery) Allow automatic detection of MTU size (possible denial of service by an attacker using a small MTU)

Setting this setting to '0' forces Windows® to use a consistent 576-byte packet size when data is transferred across a network

(NoNameReleaseOnDemand) Allow the computer to ignore NetBIOS name-release requests except from WINS servers

By default, a computer running NetBIOS will release its name upon request. In order to protect against malicious name-release attacks, set this value to '1'.

(PerformRouterDiscovery) Allow IRDP to detect and configure DefaultGateway addresses (could lead to denial of service)

This setting prohibits the workstation from caching router advertisements, preventing them from being spoofed through UDP propagation.

(SynAttackProtect) Syn attack protection level (protects against denial of service)

In order to prevent the success of a Syn attack, set the SynAttackProtect value to '2'. This allows the operating system to limit the amount of resources that are set aside until the TCP 3-way handshake is completed.

(TCPMaxConnectResponseRetransmissions) SYN-ACK retransmissions when a connection request is not acknowledged

In a typical TCP handshake, the client begins the transmission by sending a single SYN packet to the server; the server responds with a SYN-ACK packet and the client completes the handshake with an ACK packet. In some cases, the client does not respond to the server's SYN-ACK packet. This setting defines how many times the server resends the SYN-ACK packet.

Typically, the server waits three seconds after the initial packet is sent, then doubles the wait time after each successive packet. With this set to '3', the server sends the packet, waits 3 seconds, resends, waits 6 seconds, resends and waits 12 seconds before finally abandoning the connection after $3 + 6 + 12 = 21$ seconds. If this setting is set to zero, the server will wait three seconds for the client's ACK packet and then abandon the connection without resending the SYN-ACK packet

(TCPMaxDataRetransmissions) How many times unacknowledged data is retransmitted (three recommended, five is default)

This is like (TCPMaxConnectResponseRetransmissions). However, this refers to retransmission of individual data packets within an existing TCP stream.

(TCPMaxPortsExhausted) How many dropped connect requests to initiate SYN attack protection (five is recommended)

This setting defines the point at which SYN flood protection begins by measuring the number of connections that were refused because resources were not available to handle the request.

Disable autorun for all drives

Changing this setting to 255 prevents autorun initiating any applications from any drives. As the application will inherit the privileges of the user running the application, and in the case of servers this will be the administrator, this should be disabled.

Enable safe DLL search mode

This setting modifies the way in which Windows® locates driver files (.dlls). A value of '0' forces the operating system to search the current directory first; when set to '1', the system searches the Windows® system directory first.

Enable the server to stop generating 8.3 file names

This feature will force clients to reference files by their full name and not by shortened DOS-format 8.3 names.

How often keep-alive packets are send in milliseconds

The KeepAliveTime setting determines how often the network subsystem attempts to verify that a TCP session is still active. This ensures that the server does not have redundant sessions open that could be exploited for a potential attack. The recommended setting of 300,000 works out to one request every five minutes. However, this should be tested to determine the amount of traffic that this could generate on the network.

Percentage threshold at which the security event log will generate an alert

This setting determines at what stage an alert will be generated when the security log becomes full. Setting it to 70% ensures that enough time is given to alert administrators that the log is becoming full. This is especially useful in the event of an attack where the attacker is trying to overwrite the system log file to cover their activities.

The time in seconds before the screensaver grace period expires

By default, Windows® has a brief period, five seconds, between the time when the screensaver takes control of the screen and the time the system actually locks. This could allow an unauthorised user to access the system once the authorised user has stepped away from the screen.

Service settings

Care should be taken when changing settings relating to services, particularly those that are dependent on other services. Extensive testing should be done to ensure that the recommendations below are applicable to your own environment.

Permissions on services

The recommended permissions for all services are as follows:

- Administrators = Full control

- System = Full control
- Interactive = Read.

However, the above settings should be tested to ensure that they are suitable to your environment.

Alerter

The alerter service is normally used to send messages between processes on one computer 'alerting' the status of certain functions to the user's console, including the execution of print jobs. It also works in conjunction with the Messenger service to send these same messages between computers on a network.

Clipbook

The clipbook service is used to share clipboard information between computers on a network using the Network Dynamic Data Exchange (NetDDE) protocol.

Fax service

The fax service is used for the unattended reception of incoming faxes. On servers that will not provide fax services, this service should be disabled.

File replication

The file replication service (FRS) maintains a consistent file share replicated across multiple servers. If not required, it should be disabled.

FTP publishing service

The FTP publishing service is part of the Internet Information Server (IIS) suite of Internet applications and by default it is not installed on servers. If not required as part of an ISS installation, it should be disabled.

Help and support

The help and support service allows the Help and Support centre to run on the local computer. It should not be required on a server installation.

HTTP SSL

This service enables Secure Socket Layer (SSL) transport of the HTTP protocol through IIS. If not required as part of an ISS installation, it should be disabled.

IIS admin service

The IIS admin service manages the other IIS services. If this service is not running, the other services that are part of the IIS suite will not function either. This service should not be installed on servers unless they are running IIS.

Indexing service

This service indexes files on the system in an attempt to improve search performance using a flexible query language. However, the service may occasionally consume excessive resources and could theoretically be used as part of a denial-of-service attack.

License logging server

The licence monitoring service watches licensing of some Microsoft software running on the computer.

Messenger

The messenger service works in tandem with the alerter service. It allows alerter services of multiple computers to send alerts to each other over a network. It can be used to consume excessive resources on servers and networks thus causing a denial-of-service attack.

Microsoft® POP3 service

The POP3 service enables a post office protocol version 3 service on the computer. This plain-text, unencrypted protocol allows a user to retrieve messages from a mailbox. It is typically used hand in hand with the Simple Mail Transport Protocol (SMTP), necessary for sending messages.

NetMeeting remote desktop management service

As this service can be exploited by attackers to remotely connect to a system, it should be disabled on all servers and secure workstations.

Network connections

This service manages all the objects in the 'Network Connections' folder in Explorer. If set to manual, the service will automatically start when required.

Network news transport protocol (NNTP)

The NNTP service allows an IIS server to host news group discussions. If not required as part of an IIS installation, this service should be disabled.

Print spooler

Only print servers should have this service enabled.

Remote access connection manager

When attempting to access a resource on a remote network, the auto-connection manager service will automatically start the network connection when necessary. This should not be necessary for a server, since servers should have network connections permanently configured for persistent connections.

Remote access auto-connection manager

The RasMan service is necessary for creating remote network connections.

Remote administration service

The remote administration service will perform various administrative tasks requested by the remote server manager. The remote server manager service will start this when needed.

Remote desktop help session manager

This service supports the remote assistance functionality. Disable the service to prohibit the use of remote assistance.

Remote installation

The remote installation service should run only on servers used to manage client boot requests. These requests are part of the Pre-boot eXecution Environment (PXE); a remote installation server forms part of the infrastructure necessary to boot workstations from the network and push down an operating system image.

Remote procedure call (RPC) locator

This service can be used by remote clients to locate services on a remote computer.

Remote registry service

By default, the remote registry service allows remote machines to interrogate and access the registry of the servers. Disable this service to prevent remote access to the system registry.

Remote server manager

The remote server manager service uses the Windows® Management Interface (WMI) to manage remote administration alerts and tasks.

Remote server monitor

The Appmon service can monitor critical resource information on remotely managed servers.

Remote storage notification

The remote storage user link is used to notify a user when the file being accessed is only available from alternate storage media.

Remote storage server

The remote storage server service allows hierarchical storage based on storage cost and frequency of use.

Simple mail transfer protocol

This service is installed as part of the IIS suite of applications. It should be disabled or removed entirely.

Simple network management protocol (SNMP) service

If the server can be managed by a network or systems management system then this service should be disabled. Otherwise SNMP should be configured in a secure manner.

Simple network management protocol (SNMP) traps

If the server can be managed by a network or systems management system then this service should be disabled. Otherwise SNMP should be configured in a secure manner.

Telephony

The telephony service handles all the dial-up activity on the computer.

Telnet

The traffic transferred by Telnet is not protected or encrypted in any way. If this is a requirement, a secure shell (SSH) remote management solution should be employed.

Terminal services

Unless required as part of providing terminal services to clients, this service should be disabled.

Trivial FTP service

Trivial FTP (TFTP) offers a lightweight, unauthenticated version of the FTP protocol. The service is typically used for bootstrapping devices during automated start-up, and is part of the requirements for a remote installation service. This service should be disabled wherever possible.

Wireless configuration

As servers will not have wireless cards installed in them, this should be disabled.

World Wide Web publishing rights

This service should only be enabled on servers dedicated to the IIS service and managed by personnel trained in its administration and security.

User rights

Access this computer from the network

The ability to access a computer from the network is a user right that can be granted or revoked on any server as appropriate. If this list is left empty, no user accounts can be used to gain access to the resources of this computer from the network.

Act as part of the operating system

Great care should be exercised when considering using this right. The operating system works in a special security context called 'Local System'. This security context has the ability to do things which normal users and administrative users cannot. Granting this user right to users or groups will give them the ability to exceed normal privileges, regardless of their group membership.

Add workstations to the domain

This right can be assigned to users, such as support personnel to enable them to add workstations to the domain without requiring them to have full administrator permissions. By granting this right to a user account, the account will be allowed to add 10 computers to the domain.

The user receives an error when adding the eleventh computer and the action fails. In order to add an unlimited number of machines to the domain, grant users the 'create computer accounts' right for an organisational unit in Active Directory®.

Adjust memory quota for a process

This policy setting defines the accounts which can adjust the maximum amount of memory assigned to a process.

Allow to log on locally

Anyone who logs on locally to the server computer must be listed here, either by individual user name or by the 'users' group.

Allow to log on through terminal services

Although not recommended, if terminal services are enabled on the server, use this setting to explicitly control which users are allowed to remotely access the server.

Back up files and directories

This user right grants a user or group the ability to circumvent normal Windows® file security for the purposes of backing up files and folders. An account with this right will be granted read access to any file regardless of the file's access control list. It should be restricted when possible.

Bypass traverse tracking

The bypass traverse checking user right allows access to files or folders regardless of the user's permissions to the parent folder. In other words, it prevents the inheritance of permissions.

Change the system time

Changing the system time will cause all future logging to reflect the new time. This right could be used by an attacker to cover their tracks in the event logs.

Create a pagefile

In order to protect the potentially sensitive information that can be stored in a pagefile, the creation of pagefiles should be restricted to administrators.

Create a token object

This right allows the creation of a security access token. Processes requiring this right should be running under the Local System account. This right should never be given to any user.

Create global objects

Global objects are accessible to all processes running on the system. Any user able to create global objects could impact all processes running on the computer.

Create permanent shared objects

The right to create permanent shared objects should only be used by applications in the Windows® kernel. The kernel already has the right to create such objects, so no users should ever be granted this right.

Debug programs

Any user can debug his or her programs, but this right allows a user to debug other processes on a machine. Users should not be granted this right except in an isolated development environment and therefore it should never be granted to any users directly accessing the server(s).

Deny access to this computer from the network (minimum)

The 'deny access' user right always supersedes the 'allow access' user right, so if a user is listed under both user rights, that user will be denied access.

Deny logon as a batch job

Just like the other 'deny ...' user rights, a user listed here will be denied access to log on as a batch job, even if they have been explicitly granted that right.

Deny logon as a service

Just like the other 'deny ...' user rights, a user listed here will be denied access to log on as a service, even if they have been explicitly granted that right.

Deny logon locally

Just like the other 'deny ...' user rights, a user listed here will be denied access to log on to the console, even if he has been explicitly granted that right.

Deny logon through terminal services (minimum)

Similar to the other 'deny ...' rights, groups and accounts in this list will not be able to connect to the workstation using terminal services.

Enable computer and user accounts to be trusted for delegation

When a user is granted this right, they are able to change the 'trusted for delegation' setting on other domain accounts.

This setting only affects domain controllers and should not be assigned to other servers or workstations.

Force shutdown from a remote system

This grants a user the right to shut down a computer from the network. It should only be granted to administrators and indeed may be restricted to no users or groups at all.

Generate security audits

This user right allows a user or process to generate events to be added to the Windows® security event log.

Impersonate client after authentication

This right will typically be granted to a service account so it can pass the client authentication on to another service, such as a database application.

Increase scheduling priority

The scheduling priority is one of the settings that can be altered as needed for performance tuning.

Load and unload device drivers

Device drivers execute as highly privileged applications on a Windows® computer because they directly interface the hardware with the operating system. This setting actually applies to the installation of Plug and Play device drivers.

Lock pages in memory

The right to lock pages in memory is the ability to force data in physical memory to remain there and not be paged to disk, which can seriously degrade system performance. This user right is now obsolete and should remain empty.

Log on as a batch job

The right to log on as a batch job means that the listed user has the ability to log on using the batch queue facility. By default, administrators have this right, but very rarely use it. Remove all users and groups from this right.

Log on as a service

Most applications do not directly interact with the logged-on user. If a service needs to be executed in a user context, that user would have to be listed here.

Manage audit and security logs

The ability to manage the security event log is the equivalent to the ability of an intruder to cover their tracks and destroy evidence of what has been done to a computer system. This user right should be highly restricted.

Modify firmware environment values

For systems with non-volatile RAM, accounts with this privilege have the ability to modify that memory.

Perform volume maintenance tasks

The most common volume maintenance tasks are defrag and chkdsk. In addition to the potential performance impact, this right could also allow low-level access to files, bypassing standard permission constraints.

Profile system performance

This user right grants the ability for one user to monitor the performance of another user or non-system process.

Replace a process level token

The ability to replace a process level token essentially means that a process can change the authentication authority of its own child processes.

Restore files and directories

In conjunction with the 'back up files and directories' user right, this can be very dangerous if a user backs up certain security-related information, alters it and restores it back to the same place. Accounts with this privilege have owner rights access to all files, regardless of the file's access control list. It should be restricted to administrators.

Shut down the system

Users granted this right will have the ability to shut down the computer. This only takes effect if users are required to log on to shut down a system.

Synchronise directory service data

This right allows the account to read all the data in Active Directory® in order to perform synchronisation. Only the System account on domain controllers should have this right.

Take ownership of file or other object

A user who 'owns' a file has greater authority over that file than even the permissions would suggest. The right to take ownership of a file is equivalent to the ability to compromise an entire file system.

File system permissions

File permissions are used to limit access to sensitive programs. Often file permissions provide a final layer of protection to prevent an attacker from gaining or elevating access on the system.

Registry permissions

The registry contains many sensitive settings which control the behaviour of almost all aspects of the system and its applications. The operating system allows specific access controls to be placed on each registry folder, similar to permissions on file folders.

File and registry auditing

Auditing of file systems and registry settings can be an invaluable tool when investigating a potential compromise and identifying what is happening or has happened. However, there is a performance overhead on the system and also an impact on the size of the log files. The recommendations in this document may address the latter but you will need to determine the impact versus benefit of the former.

APPENDIX 2: BIBLIOGRAPHY, REFERENCE AND FURTHER READING

ISO27001 resources

Standalone ISO27001 ISMS Toolkit (ITGP)
www.itgovernance.co.uk/shop/p-1462.aspx

IT Governance: An international guide to data security and ISO27001/ISO27002
www.itgovernance.co.uk/shop/p-772.aspx

Nine Steps to Success: an ISO27001 Implementation Overview
www.itgovernance.co.uk/shop/p-963.aspx

Information Security Risk Management for ISO27001/ISO27002
www.itgovernance.co.uk/shop/p-607.aspx

Microsoft resources

Windows Server® 2012 Security Guide
http://technet.microsoft.com/en-us/library/jj898542.aspx

Windows Server® 2008 Security Guide
http://technet.microsoft.com/en-us/library/cc264463.aspx

Windows Server® 2003 Security Guide
http://technet.microsoft.com/en-us/library/cc163140.aspx

Microsoft® Windows® Security
www.microsoft.com/security

Microsoft Threats and Countermeasures Guide
technet.microsoft.com/en-us/library/dd162275.aspx

Appendix 2: Bibliography, Reference and Further Reading

Configuring Outlook Security Features to Help Prevent Viruses
http://office.microsoft.com/en-us/ork2003/HA011402911033.aspx

How to use Microsoft® Baseline Security Advisor
http://msdn.microsoft.com/en-us/library/aa302360.aspx

Microsoft® Security Compliance Manager
http://technet.microsoft.com/en-us/library/cc677002.aspx

Microsoft® Office® 2007 Security Guide
http://technet.microsoft.com/en-us/library/cc500475.aspx

Microsoft® Windows® 8 Security Baseline
http://technet.microsoft.com/en-us/library/jj916413.aspx

Microsoft® Windows® 7 Security Baseline
http://technet.microsoft.com/en-us/library/ee712767.aspx

Microsoft Security Guidance
http://technet.microsoft.com/en-us/library/cc184906.aspx

Data Encryption Toolkit for Mobile PCs
http://technet.microsoft.com/en-us/library/cc500474.aspx

Microsoft Security Risk Management Guide
http://technet.microsoft.com/en-us/library/cc163143.aspx

Security Monitoring and Attack Detection Planning Guide
http://technet.microsoft.com/library/cc163158.aspx.

The Microsoft Security Response Center Blog
http://blogs.technet.com/b/msrc/

Microsoft products

Microsoft® Windows Server® 2012
www.microsoft.com/en-us/server-cloud/products/windows-server-2012-r2/default.aspx

Microsoft® Windows® 8
http://windows.microsoft.com/en-gb/windows-8/meet

Microsoft® Antigen
www.microsoft.com/en-gb/download/details.aspx?id=8138

Microsoft® Forefront™ Technologies
http://technet.microsoft.com/en-us/forefront/ff899332

Microsoft® Forefront™ Threat Management Gateway
www.microsoft.com/forefront/threat-management-gateway/en/us/overview.aspx

Microsoft® System Center
www.microsoft.com/en-us/server-cloud/products/system-center-2012-r2/default.aspx

Microsoft® Windows Server® Update Services
http://technet.microsoft.com/en-ie/wsus/default(en-us).aspx

Microsoft® Source Code Analyzer for SQL Injection
www.microsoft.com/en-us/download/details.aspx?id=16305

Microsoft® Threat Analysis and Modeling
www.microsoft.com/en-us/download/details.aspx?id=14719

Microsoft® Baseline Security Analyzer
http://technet.microsoft.com/en-ie/security/cc184923(en-us).aspx

Microsoft® Security Assessment Tool
http://technet.microsoft.com/en-us/security/cc297183

Microsoft Log Parser
www.microsoft.com/en-us/download/details.aspx?id=24659

Other resources

The Center for Internet Security
www.cisecurity.org

The SANS Institute
www.sans.org

USA National Institute of Standards and Technology
http://csrc.nist.gov/publications

ITG RESOURCES

IT Governance Ltd sources, creates and delivers products and services to meet the real-world, evolving IT governance needs of today's organisations, directors, managers and practitioners.

The ITG website (_www.itgovernance.co.uk_) is the international one-stop-shop for corporate and IT governance information, advice, guidance, books, tools, training and consultancy. On the website you will find the following page related to the subject matter of this book:

www.itgovernance.co.uk/iso27001.aspx.

Publishing Services

IT Governance Publishing (ITGP) is the world's leading IT-GRC publishing imprint that is wholly owned by IT Governance Ltd.

With books and tools covering all IT governance, risk and compliance frameworks, we are the publisher of choice for authors and distributors alike, producing unique and practical publications of the highest quality, in the latest formats available, which readers will find invaluable.

www.itgovernancepublishing.co.uk is the website dedicated to ITGP. Other titles published by ITGP that may be of interest include:

- Nine Steps to Success: An ISO27001:2013 Implementation Overview

  www.itgovernance.co.uk/shop/p-963-nine-steps-to-success-an-iso-270012013-implementation-overview-second-edition.aspx

- CyberWar, CyberTerror, CyberCrime and CyberActivism

www.itgovernance.co.uk/shop/p-511-cyberwar-cyberterror-cybercrime-and-cyberactivism-second-edition.aspx

- Penetration Testing: Protecting Networks and Systems

  www.itgovernance.co.uk/shop/p-1024-penetration-testing-protecting-networks-and-systems.aspx.

We also offer a range of off-the-shelf toolkits that give comprehensive, customisable documents to help users create the specific documentation they need to properly implement a management system or standard. Written by experienced practitioners and based on the latest best practice, ITGP toolkits can save months of work for organisations working towards compliance with a given standard.

For further information please review the following pages:

- ISO27001 2013 ISMS Standalone Documentation Toolkit

  www.itgovernance.co.uk/shop/p-1462.aspx

- Full range of toolkits

  www.itgovernance.co.uk/shop/c-129-toolkits.aspx.

Books and tools published by IT Governance Publishing (ITGP) are available from all business booksellers and the following websites:

www.itgovernance.eu   *www.itgovernanceusa.com*

www.itgovernance.in   *www.itgovernancesa.co.za*

www.itgovernance.asia.

Training Services

IT Governance offers an extensive portfolio of training courses designed to educate information security, IT governance, risk management and compliance professionals. Our classroom and online training programmes will help you develop the skills required to deliver best practice and compliance to your organisation. They will also enhance your career by providing you with industry standard certifications and increased peer recognition. Our range of courses offer a structured learning path from Foundation to Advanced level in the key topics of information security, IT governance, business continuity and service management.

ISO/IEC 27001:2013 is the international management standard that helps businesses and organisations throughout the world develop a best-in-class Information Security Management System (ISMS). Knowledge and experience in implementing and maintaining ISO27001 compliance are considered to be essential to building a successful career in information security. We have the world's first programme of certificated ISO27001 education with Foundation, Lead Implementer, Risk Management and Lead Auditor training courses. Each course is designed to provide delegates with relevant knowledge and skills and an industry-recognised qualification awarded by the International Board for IT Governance Qualifications (IBITGQ).

Full details of all IT Governance training courses can be found at www.itgovernance.co.uk/training.aspx.

Professional Services and Consultancy

Your mission to plug critical security gaps will be greatly assisted by IT Governance consultants, who have advised hundreds of information security managers in the adoption of ISO27001 information security management systems (ISMS).

At IT Governance, we understand that information, information security and information technology are always business issues, and not just IT ones. Our consultancy services assist you in managing information security strategies in harmony with business goals, conveying the right messages to your colleagues to support decision-making.

The organisation's assets, security and data systems, not to mention its reputation, are all in your hands. A major security breach could spell disaster. Timely advice and support from IT Governance expert consultants could make all the difference, enabling you to identify risks and put the necessary controls in place before there's a need to respond to a serious incident.

For more information about ISO27001 consultancy from IT Governance Ltd, see:

www.itgovernance.co.uk/consulting.aspx.

Newsletter

IT governance is one of the hottest topics in business today, not least because it is also the fastest moving.

You can stay up to date with the latest developments across the whole spectrum of IT governance subject matter, including; risk management, information security, ITIL and IT service management, project governance, compliance and so much more, by subscribing to ITG's core publications and topic alert emails.

Simply visit our subscription centre and select your preferences: *www.itgovernance.co.uk/newsletter.aspx.*

EU for product safety is Stephen Evans, The Mill Enterprise Hub, Stagreenan, Drogheda, Co. Louth, A92 CD3D, Ireland. (servicecentre@itgovernance.eu)

www.ingramcontent.com/pod-product-compliance
Lightning Source LLC
LaVergne TN
LVHW022302060326
832902LV00020B/3218